20

CELEBRATING TWO DECADES OF CHANGED LIVES

CREDITS

The Message Story
Written by: Andy Hawthorne
Copy Editor: Craig Borlase

20 Stories
Editor: Alistair Metcalfe

Production Team
Project Manager: Ian Rowbottom
Art Director: Dan Hasler
Graphic Design: Bethan Wilson
Proofreader: Dev Lunsford

ISBN: 978-0-9571414-0-7

PHOTOGRAPHY:
Howard Barlow, Martin Butcher, Dan Hasler, Sam Hawthorne,
Joe Kizlauskas, Katy Lunsford, Jonathan Mark, Gemma Marriner,
Bruce Marshall, Christina Otoo-Anakwa, Ian Rowbottom, Alan Saunders,
Kerry Slater, Lucy Smith, Cat Taylor, Lucy West, Matt Wilson

See, I am doing a new thing!
Now it springs up; do you not perceive it?

Isaiah 43:19

CONTENTS

FRIENDS

TWENTY STORIES

FOREWORD
LUIS PALAU

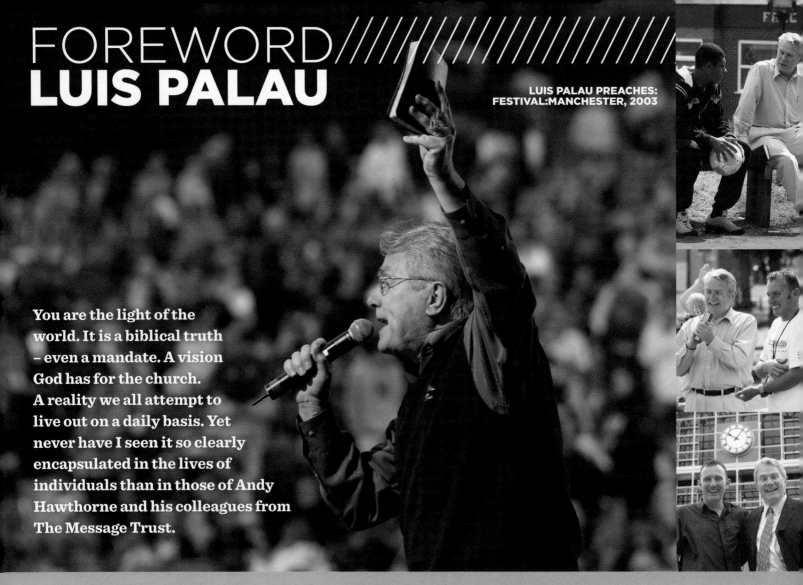

LUIS PALAU PREACHES:
FESTIVAL:MANCHESTER, 2003

You are the light of the world. It is a biblical truth – even a mandate. A vision God has for the church. A reality we all attempt to live out on a daily basis. Yet never have I seen it so clearly encapsulated in the lives of individuals than in those of Andy Hawthorne and his colleagues from The Message Trust.

It is sheer delight to speak a good word for the great ministry of The Message. So much has happened since its inception I can hardly believe it has only been 20 years.

From the first time we heard about the ministry of The Message, we were immediately fascinated. We began to pray for the movement and for the members of the Trust. We have had the joy of ministering together in various cities of the UK. And we've watched the Lord use these servants of God in wonderful ways. God's blessing has clearly been on their work and few things have brought me as much joy as working together with these bold, evangelistic servants of our God on High.

The sacrificial ministry of the workers who have devoted themselves to live in very risky and yet needy areas of Greater Manchester has moved us deeply. It has challenged us in tremendous ways. Their servant hearts – proclaiming the Good News throughout Manchester and the UK – has resulted

TOP:
LUIS TALKS WITH A YOUNG PERSON DURING F:M

MIDDLE:
LUIS AND ANDY CHECKING OUT ONE OF HUNDREDS OF F:M PROJECTS.

BOTTOM:
LUIS & ANDY AT THE LAUNCH OF F:M

in tens of thousands of changed lives. And it has blessed me no end.

It has been a true delight to minister with Andy, his wife Michele, and the team over the years. Praying. Strategising. Vision-casting. Dreaming. As we have sat together in various cities throughout the world I have come to realise that I have much to learn from these young, talented followers of Christ.

We at the Luis Palau Association have picked up on many unique and powerful ministry models started by The Message. They have helped revolutionise our ministry all across the world. The whole concept of service and showing the love of Christ – paralleled with out and out evangelisation – has had an impact beyond our imagination.

Over the years, the Luis Palau Association has incorporated many principles that we learned from The Message into our overall city-wide evangelisation. We aim – like the Trust in the UK – to reach whole cities with the good news of Jesus Christ. We also aim to serve the community as Jesus indicated in Matthew 5:16 – "Let your light shine before others, that they may see your good deeds and glorify your Father in heaven."

A city cannot only hear the good news. They must also see the effects of it in action – house to house and neighbourhood by neighbourhood.

> *We've watched the Lord use these servants of God in wonderful ways. God's blessing has clearly been on their work*

That is what I have learned from The Message. And frankly, it was one of the great thrills of our lives.

Now there are hundreds or thousands – probably even millions – across the Spanish-speaking world, the United States of America, France, and Asia who are thanking God without knowing the source. Our models were born from The Message... the pure example of Andy Hawthorne and the others.

We pray that the next 20 years will be even more fruitful; that the ministry of the Trust will expand far beyond and that many young people will be challenged to be a blessing to cities around the world as a fruit of this ministry.

This story – as it is told by Andy, who is such an enthusiastic servant of God – will encourage any believer. It will challenge your commitment to Christ. It will push you toward the exciting life of evangelism. And it will instil in you a life of service.

May God bless the Trust in tremendous ways.

Luis Palau, Evangelist

CHAPTER ONE

Belts, Braces and the Start of the Journey

**ABOVE:
ANDY & SIMON
HAWTHORNE,
TAKEN FROM THE
PROGRAMME FOR
MESSAGE '88**

What you're holding in your hands is a celebration of twenty fantastic years of God having his way in the greatest city on earth. But the truth about the story is that it starts even earlier than August 1992 and begins even before the birth of The Message Trust. This one starts in Manchester in 1987 and it involves me, my brother and lots of pairs of braces.

It was all Lady Diana's fault. My brother Simon and I had been selling various fashion accessories and doing OK, until we got hold of these braces – or suspenders if you happen to live on the other side of the Atlantic. They were the exact ones that Lady Diana had started wearing, and we couldn't shift them fast enough. Business was booming and we needed more employees fast.

Our factory was based in inner-city Manchester for no better reason than that's where we could get the biggest grants and the lowest rent. But God clearly had a greater plan in mind than boosting our profits, and when the local jobcentre discovered that we had a really poor recruitment procedure they started to send us all the lads they couldn't place anywhere else.

So there we were with all these young lads who had just come out of the local young offenders' institutions or had got sacked by every other local employer. Not only were they hopeless at making braces, there was graffiti, vandalism, violence and theft. This was all very distressing, but the worst of it was that they seemed to know nothing of Christ. Simon and I were shocked that no one was sharing the gospel with them either through words or actions.

> ❝ They seemed to know nothing of Christ. Simon and I were shocked that no one was sharing the gospel with them ❞

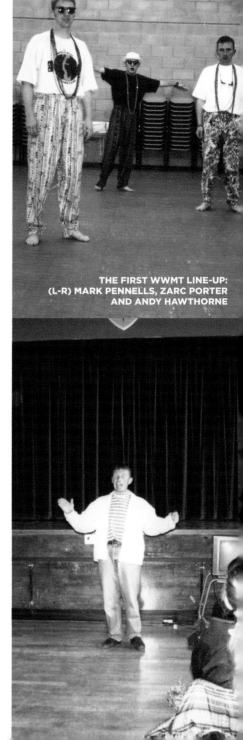

**THE FIRST WWMT LINE-UP:
(L-R) MARK PENNELLS, ZARC PORTER
AND ANDY HAWTHORNE**

**RIGHT:
ANDY PREACHES
IN SCHOOL**

Maybe we shouldn't have been surprised. After all, the churches around the factory were the sort that met behind barbed wire fences with the alarm on whilst lads like the ones we employed chucked bricks through the windows. So much for church in the community.

The largest church on the estate stood about 50 yards from our factory, but long ago it had been shut down and sold to a knitwear manufacturer. We'd go in there from time to time, dropping off the jumpers we'd embroidered (yes, we also did that). Where the pews used to be, there were knitting machines rattling away but still above the choir stalls in gold leaf it read: 'Without a vision, the people perish'. If ever there was a prophetic word for inner-city Manchester, this was it. It's not that there never had been Christians with God-given vision: hundreds of years ago they sacrificed so much of what they had to build beautiful church buildings. Sadly, somewhere along the road they had lost the vision of being the Jesus-honouring, Bible-believing, community-transforming church that the area so desperately needed.

Anyway, by the time April 1987 came around business was booming. Simon and I were at a local fashion trade show and we got talking about everything. Yes, our staff were a little scrappy, but we were doing well. But was that it? Wasn't there something else we should be doing besides giving these lads a job? As we talked, something happened. We felt as though we had something extra special straight from God himself: vision. We hatched a plan. It was probably a bit arrogant – and it was certainly naive of us – but we decided to write to

all 1100 church leaders in Greater Manchester and set them a challenge. There were so many young people with so many needs – would these churches put on their own events to start reaching out to them? If they'd do their bit then Simon and I would book what was then the biggest rock venue in Manchester – The Apollo Theatre – not for one night, but for a full week of credible Christian outreach events with the best bands, theatre companies and special guests.

This was wacky faith stuff, but we rode that buzz of initial excitement for all it was worth. A couple of hours later I got home and every ounce of faith seemed to drain right out of me. I heard a little voice saying: "Who do you think you are? You've not got the resources, gifts or experience to pull that off, you'll be laughed at!" It's a voice I've come to recognise these days, and I can deal with it better today. Yet back then I prayed hard and said, "Please, God, if this idea is really from you, will you confirm it over the next days?" I wish I'd had the bottle to ask him to speak to me right then because right after praying that desperate prayer I opened my Bible and read my set reading for the day, Isaiah 43:18–21:

"Forget the former things; do not dwell on the past. See, I am doing a new thing! Now it springs up; do you not perceive it? I am making a way in the wilderness and streams in the wasteland. The wild animals honour me, the jackals and the owls, because I provide water in the wilderness and streams in the wasteland, to give drink to my people, my chosen, the people I formed for myself that they may proclaim my praise."

I don't think there are actually any better or more relevant verses anywhere in the Bible that I could have read back then. They remain the touchstone words upon which everything we do is built, and 25 years on you will see them prominently displayed around our headquarters.

It's a beautiful thought that some of these lads who we had been employing – the ones who definitely fitted the wild animal description that Isaiah wrote – were actually formed to declare God's praises and go from being the problem to being the answer. It's a promise we've seen fulfilled over and over again in the intervening years.

After the letter went out to the church leaders, something amazing happened. Around 300 local missions took place in the build-up to the week at The Apollo, and by the end of the whole thing many thousands of young people had heard the good news in language they could understand. By the final night they were starting to queue up at 2.30pm just to get in. Loads of young people became Christians and signed up for Just Looking groups, and it was also so encouraging to see churches praying and working together in a way that, as far as we knew, hadn't happened for generations. It wasn't just us who were excited – the local churches were pumped and encouraged us to do it all again, next Christmas.

That was Message '88, and we took the church leaders up on their challenge and rolled out Christmas Message '89 the following year. Through both of them we experienced the gut-wrenching business of praying in the

BELOW: ANDY WITH A LOCAL YOUTH GROUP AFTER MESSAGE '88

finances, and on each occasion it wasn't until the very last minute that the money came in. As we celebrate our 20th Anniversary we have seen the Lord provide well over £25 million for this work, but still so much of it arrives just at the last minute. And, yes, I still get stressed at times like these, but I know for sure that the Lord seems to love to teach us big lessons about trust and dependence through this way of operating. And I'm glad he does.

After all the fun and games of '88 and '89 we thought that it might be time to get back to the serious business of manufacturing novelty belts and braces. Fortunately, God had other ideas and during 1990 a musician called Mark Pennells approached Simon and me with an idea for something he suggested we could call 'Message to Schools'. He wanted to go into local schools and use his pop music as a way in with me preaching and teaching about the Christian faith alongside him. By now I'd found that I had a serious bug for evangelism, particularly in inner-city schools, so I didn't take much convincing. We spent 1990 fundraising and scheming for 1991 when Message to Schools was finally launched with a week in Cheadle Hulme High School.

We ran lessons, assemblies and lunchtime meetings that all culminated in a Friday concert in their largest assembly hall. Seventy-five kids turned up, all of them looking completely bored. Mark did his music and I did my best to preach as if there were thousands of them out there. At the end we invited them to join Mark and me in the changing room to receive Christ. You know what? Thirty-nine spiritually hungry young people did just that! And that night a ministry was born. Twenty years on we've seen literally tens of thousands of young people make that world-shaking, eternity-defining step. Life doesn't get any better.

> " By the end of the whole thing many thousands of young people had heard the good news in language they could understand "

GAIL BALLANCE

I am so grateful to have heard *about Jesus*

I became a Christian at the very first Message event in October 1988. I was working as a student nurse at Wythenshawe Hospital when a friend I met on a ward invited me to the gig at the Apollo in Manchester.

I was living in the nurses' home and feeling vulnerable because I had recently left home. Just a year before that I had lost my father to a tragic accident. So I was searching for God and knew I needed something in my life. I had always believed in God but was not sure how real he was. My best friend at that time was a Jehovah's Witness and I was doing studies with her about what they believed.

I went to the Message event with an open mind but during the week it soon became confused. I knew I was going to have to make a decision whether I believed the things my Jehovah's Witness friend said about Jesus or what I was hearing at the Message.

I am so grateful to have heard about Jesus in an atmosphere that was real and relevant back then. The presentation of the Gospel was exciting and tangible but most of all made sense. On the last night of the Message I gave my life to Jesus and became a Christian.

Looking back, what an amazing adventure I've had! My life has been enriched having made that crucial decision all those years ago. I can stand back and say how God has been with me throughout all of life's trials and joys – in my marriage, bringing up my daughter, the passion he has given me for pregnant women in Africa.

I've seen miracles happening in my challenging but rewarding job as a midwife and I know that it's only by having Jesus at my side that I am able to do the job. God gets me through this on a day-to-day basis.

I really cannot imagine my life not being a Christian. Oh, and the friend who took me along? He's been my beloved husband for 20 years.

story 01

So thank you to Andy and Simon Hawthorne who listened to God all those years ago, took that vision forward and allowed God to use them to reach people and change lives like mine.

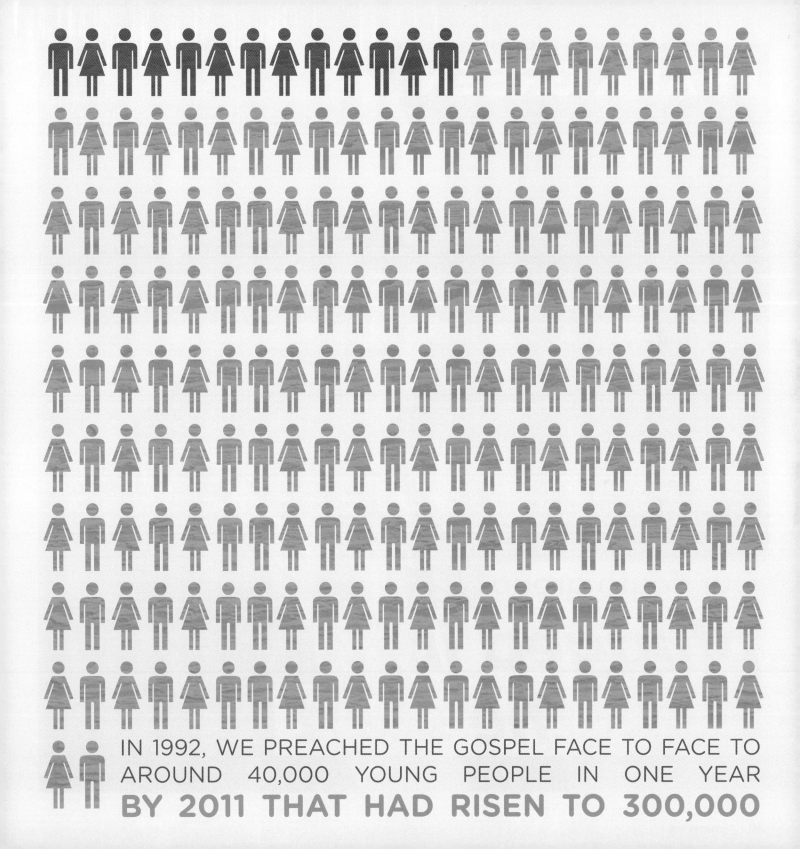

IN 1992, WE PREACHED THE GOSPEL FACE TO FACE TO
AROUND 40,000 YOUNG PEOPLE IN ONE YEAR
BY 2011 THAT HAD RISEN TO 300,000

FRANK GREEN

Our youth group
plugged in
from the start

I was a rookie Youth Pastor at Altrincham Baptist Church when Andy and Simon came up with the idea of holding a weekend of evangelistic concerts at The Apollo. The weekend was the climax of months of mini youth missions all around the city with local bands like Except For Access and a theatre group from Cheadle called Double Vision!

This was a very new and exciting approach to evangelism which really communicated effectively to teenagers. The bands and actors were excellent role models who not only got the gospel message across in the language of the day but also dressed like normal young people and clearly enjoyed living for Jesus. A very attractive and convincing alternative to the hedonistic values of most who take to the stage to perform their art.

Today when I look around the staff and volunteers involved with The Message, I see exactly the same as then, just on a larger scale. Talented, highly committed young people who connect so relevantly and effectively with their peers and whose whole life focus is on reaching lost young people for Christ.

Our youth group plugged in from the start of Message '88: we held prayer evenings and evangelism training courses, we joined in with events run by other youth groups around the city, went out into the town centre on Saturday mornings doing open-air drama, sketch-boarding and boldly preaching the good news to shoppers and passers-by. It was a very exciting time for us and by the time the Apollo event arrived the Youth Fellowship had grown from 50 to about 80, most of the newcomers being unchurched friends of the existing members.

We took over 100 teenagers to the big gigs and many made first-time commitments to Christ. Most continued in their faith and grew into strong and effective believers, many taking on leadership roles in university CU groups around the UK in the ensuing years. I am still in touch with a good number of them to this day – we recently held a reunion and Message '88 featured prominently in many of the conversations on the night.

I remember writing to Andy and Simon after the weekend to encourage them for their creative and ambitious venture, and thinking what a great way this was to reach young people with the gospel – the medium of pop music and theatre being so central in the life of today's teens. Looking back over the years, it seems like God had similar thoughts!

CHAPTER TWO

Finding the Big Wave

Recently I went to speak at Hillsong Church in Moscow. Now the very fact there is a Hillsong Church in Moscow is a miracle in itself. I remember as a baby Christian praying hard for Christians who were being persecuted behind the Iron Curtain and if you'd told me then that years later I would be freely preaching at a loud, lively and relevant church in Moscow – and that lots of young people there would become Christians – I'd have been amazed.

When I arrived the pastor excitedly got his phone out and started to play *Jumping in the House of God.*

"This music kept me going when I'd just become a Christian," he said in broken English.

Again I was stunned. I'm not a musician, dancer or rapper and I would never have thought that the tunes we were making for Manchester schoolies would encourage people all over the world.

Alongside Isaiah 43:18–21, another one of our much-quoted verses at The Message is 2 Chronicles 16:9:

"For the eyes of the Lord range throughout the earth to strengthen those whose hearts are fully committed to him."

Do you know what God's looking for? It's simple: heart. A heart for him and a heart for his world. He doesn't need the richest, sexiest, most gifted people to get the job done; he just wants people with a heart. I believe that's what God saw in the early days of Message to Schools – a heart for Manchester, for lost young people, for unity and for his Word, the Bible. When

> **Do you know what God's looking for? It's simple: heart. A heart for him and a heart for his world**

God sees those things he tends to lend his strong support, and that's exactly what happened when it all started to kick off with our funny little band called The World Wide Message Tribe.

The plan for Message to Schools was that Mark would do the music and I would do the preaching. It was a formula that worked pretty well, but at some time during 1991 it began to change. We were in the studio with our producer Zarc Porter, just throwing a few ideas around for Mark's next songs. For some reason I started doing some jokey gravelly-style rapping. To my surprise Mark and Zarc loved it and we quickly recorded some of this rapping on Mark's next song. Next time we were doing a gig in school we performed it together and the kids went mad for it. Maybe we were on to something?

We recorded more and more stuff with my strange rapping style against these trippy beats. As we travelled around the schools we also recruited a couple of singers – namely Elaine Hanley and Lorraine Williams – as well as some dancers from Mark's youth group. We realised we were now a band and so we gave ourselves the name The World Wide Message Tribe. It was a strange name for a band who were totally focused on Manchester, but we liked it.

ANDY AND CAMERON TAKE A SCHOOLS LESSON

For a while in the early 90s Manchester seemed like the centre of the global music scene. Dance music was everywhere so we decided to milk this for the gospel. Zarc started producing tracks that actually sounded credible and chart-worthy, unlike much of the cheesy Christian music that was around at the time. It was an exhilarating time as suddenly thousands, rather than hundreds, of kids turned up at our gigs and as a result many thousands came to know Christ.

News about this funny schools band also started to travel around the world and eventually record companies and large concert promoters started to take an interest. We made a decision that Manchester schools and church partnership would always be our focus and that anything else that came along, no matter how large and prestigious, would have to fit in with this. We also decided that any royalties we might make from the gigs and recordings would be ploughed straight back into the work. I'm convinced that these two decisions left God free to bless and open doors for the band.

We signed a record deal with Warners on the strict understanding that we couldn't tour and promote our albums like other bands. For several years we lived the schizophrenic lifestyle of working hard in schools during term time and then going off around the world and being treated a bit like pop stars during school breaks.

All this meant that in 1993, after we formed The Message Trust, I left the business I'd started with Simon so that I could focus all my attention on ducking and diving in order to reach as many young people as possible.

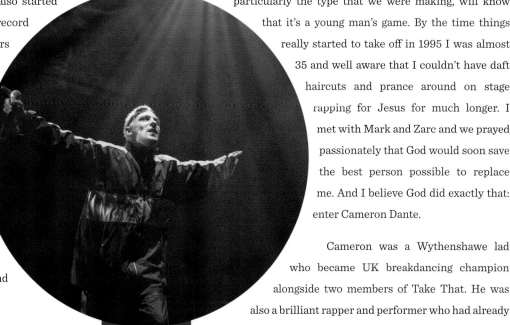

CAMERON DANTE AT PLANET LIFE

For the first two or three years The World Wide Message Tribe was our main source of income. Now twenty years on, less than 5% of our finances comes through royalties and gig fees and so much of the rest comes to us through the thousands of faithful friends of this ministry that we have picked up over the years.

I'll admit that it was exciting to sense the buzz being created all over the world by The World Wide Message Tribe, but anyone who knows anything about pop music, particularly the type that we were making, will know that it's a young man's game. By the time things really started to take off in 1995 I was almost 35 and well aware that I couldn't have daft haircuts and prance around on stage rapping for Jesus for much longer. I met with Mark and Zarc and we prayed passionately that God would soon save the best person possible to replace me. And I believe God did exactly that: enter Cameron Dante.

Cameron was a Wythenshawe lad who became UK breakdancing champion alongside two members of Take That. He was also a brilliant rapper and performer who had already had several hits with the dance outfit Bizarre, Inc. Alongside this went a crazy lifestyle of drugs and clubbing so when he came to record in Zarc's studio we committed to praying for him every day. Bit by bit – mainly due to Zarc's witness – Cameron was drawn to Jesus. One night we finally managed to get him to our Planet Life event which by now had become the largest regular youth celebration event the city had ever seen. On that very first night he went to the front and fully surrendered his life to Christ.

Suddenly his lyrics were not about sex and drugs but about his relationship with Jesus. God had both answered our prayers and ripped our new World Wide Message Tribe front man right out of the world. I may be biased but I don't think I have ever seen a more magnetic performer than Cameron at his best, and combined with the fact that he was a quite awesomely gifted evangelist, the whole thing was taken to another level.

We became more and more of a worldwide tribe. We decided to work more as a collective rather than a traditional band, and over the next decade we went through various incarnations and worked with some awesome people. There was Sani from Swaziland, the amazing Deronda Lewis from the buckle of the Bible belt in Texas, plus the lovable Tim and Emma Owen and of course Lindsay West and lots more singers, dancers, and rappers who all carried the same passion for Manchester, the church, the Bible, and the lost.

The band sold hundreds of thousands of albums and performed face to face to well over a million young people. We became the first UK band to have a number one Christian radio single in the States and even won three Dove awards for our efforts. All the time we stayed focused on our mission to Manchester schools, learning the truth behind the wisdom that ministry is a little like surfing: you try and get up but end up exhausted. Then, just when your eyes are stinging and your throat is sore, a big wave comes along and carries you a very long way in a very short space of time.

I hope it doesn't sound too arrogant to say that our 'big wave' in those early days which carried us so far forwards in such a short space of time was The World Wide Message Tribe. Even with the rapper who sounded like a demonised member of Sesame Street, God used that band as the foundation for so much that has grown and developed over the last twenty years.

> " The band sold hundreds of thousands of albums and performed face to face to well over a million young people "

JENNY BROWN

I didn't totally understand
what I was signing up for
***but I knew that
I needed God***

I grew up in a small house in Salford with my mum, dad and seven siblings. Where we lived was one of those places where people never wanted to park their car. Drug and gun crimes were not uncommon. None of my family were Christians – my sister and I went to church at Christmas and Easter but that was it.

On the October 30, 1999, at the age of 12, I attended a concert which followed a week where The World Wide Message Tribe had led all the RE lessons in my school.

Towards the end of the evening, Deronda from the Tribe sang a song and we were all asked to listen to the words and watch a video where Christ was crucified. After the song we were asked if we wanted to become a Christian. To be honest, I didn't totally understand what I was signing up for but I knew that I needed God and he would help me if I went and prayed that prayer.

Afterwards I got chatting to a lady from the Eden team who helped me understand what I had done and invited me their church the next day. So that Sunday I went along. The same lady was waiting for me, and after a little while the church became my spiritual home.

A little time after that the LifeCentre opened and I took part in all the activities: I remember 24-hour prayer sessions in the loft, learning how to be a DJ and how to touch-type. Most of all I remember Michele Hawthorne's arts and crafts. In December 2001, after lots of love, encouragement and support, I felt ready to take the plunge and be baptised.

In the years that followed, I became a volunteer on the Message's Eden Bus which I use to go on as a kid. I also began volunteering at The Message's major events in the summer.

I am very thankful for the work of The Message. I still remember everything that happened when I was a brand new Christian, including the letters I used to receive from Emma Owen, another member of the Tribe. Her letters taught me how to deal with things in life, and how to become more like Christ. Everything I learnt from Emma and others is still with me and influences my walk with God. The decision I made 12 years ago was the best decision of my life.

story
03

the big chill
AT ALTRINCHAM ICE RINK

PLANET LIFE

massive new Planet Life radical worship servi...

The World Wide Message Tribe · Cameron Dan...
Tribal Expression · Andy Hawthorne and more

At the Manchester Apollo Theatre, Stockport Road,
Ardwick, Manchester, M12

All seats £2

October 17th, November 21st,
December 19th

The Message · PO Box 14 · CHEADLE · SK8 2FE
0161 491 5400 · Fax 0161 491 5400 · info@message.org.uk
www.message.org.uk · Please make cheques payable to The Message

B E

BY THE END OF 2012
WE WILL HAVE TRAINED & RELEASED OVER

400 URBAN & CREATIVE EVANGELISTS

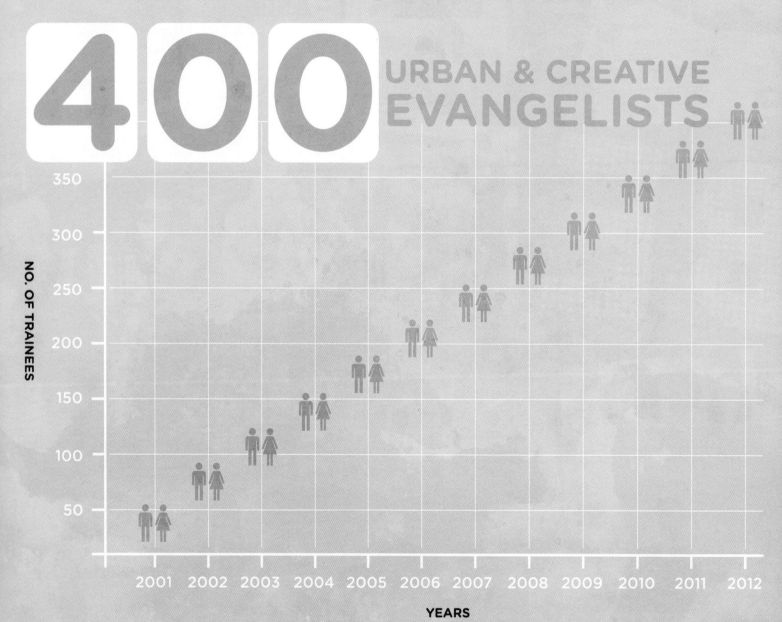

NO. OF TRAINEES

350

300

250

200

150

100

50

2001 2002 2003 2004 2005 2006 2007 2008 2009 2010 2011 2012

YEARS

If you want to get some idea of just how special the ministry entrusted to The Message is, all you need do is visit one of their monthly prayer days. I've had the privilege of being at a couple of these recently, and it's one of the most faith-building environments you can ever imagine.

Matt & Beth *Redman*

Throughout the day various team members report back on what's been happening in schools, young offenders' institutions and Eden projects. There's story after story of rescue, breakthrough and transformation in even the hardest of hearts, or the toughest of situations.

If this were just a one-off event it would be inspiring enough in and of itself. But as wonderful and wowing as they are, these reports are simply the fruit of the most recent month of ministry. If you visit more than once, you'll start to get a picture of just how special what's happening throughout Manchester and the surrounding areas is. For every single time, the stories flooding in are just as compelling and as numerous as the month before.

The astounding thing is that this has now been going on, in some shape or form, for 20 years. It's hard to fathom just how many lives will have been touched in some way by the gospel of Jesus Christ through the reaching-out of The Message in these couple of decades. And who can tell what lies ahead? Being around this ministry, you can't help but think that the best is still yet to come.

MATT REDMAN,
SONGWRITER AND WORSHIP LEADER

Being a part of The Message was without doubt one of the best experiences of my life.

We prayed, we fasted, we evangelised, we laughed, we travelled, we learned, we sowed, we reaped and we grew as a result! It was an unforgettable two years for me!

Andy Hawthorne and The Message team in Manchester changed my life. They are, without doubt, not only real-deal Christians, passionate and utterly God centred, but they are, I believe, the best schools workers in Britain! They also knew how to disciple us as well as train and stretch us! I still pinch myself that I got to be a part of the Big Vision in Manchester.

What more can I say?

BETH REDMAN,
SONGWRITER AND AUTHOR

DERONDA LEWIS

proclaiming *Jesus is Lord!*

Just thinking about my time at The Message makes me smile. When leaving America to move to the UK, I was not at all sure what to expect.

Anyone who knows me knows I come from a strong black gospel background and this is not what I found in Manchester. The first concert (with the loud thumping music) almost sent me right back to the good old USA. However, I prayed and felt like I was supposed to stay right where I was.

One thing that helped was that I joined The World Wide Message Tribe at the same time a lovely young couple was brought in, Tim and Emma Owen. The three of us formed a great bond working our way into the group.

During my early days, I often thought God had a great sense of humour in bringing me completely out of my comfort zone. I now know that he was teaching me a great lesson, showing me that ministry comes in all forms and fashions, yes – fashions. Some of the clothes and hairstyles kind of took me over the top. However, when I saw how the kids loved it and it gave the group a platform to speak to them, I just thought, "do your thing Jesus!"

My time in the UK gave me some of the wettest days of my life, some brilliant times of ministry, a lifetime of memories and definitely some of the best friends I'll ever have. Looking back, I have to say "thank you, Jesus" for using a bunch of funny-hair mad people to show me you can work outside the box.

Today, I'm back into my gospel. I still travel a bit (and I do add a little 'thump' in from time to time). I am also the proud president of a women's support group called B.I.G. The group is designed to help women overcome weight issues, insecurities (emotional and physical) and build self-esteem. Wherever I am or whatever I'm doing, I'm still proclaiming that Jesus is Lord!

story 04

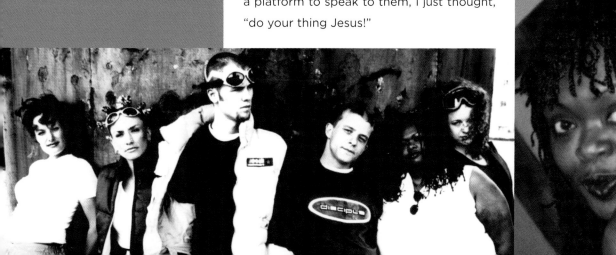

CHAPTER THREE

The Streets of Eden

It's 1996 and the work of The Message Trust is growing rapidly. We're able to develop some resources, which we call *Get God* and we're using them to help local churches disciple the hundreds of young people who are committing their lives to Christ at the school gigs. But while this is good, we know it's nowhere near enough. If we're truly going to help the damaged and dysfunctional young people floating around the inner city, we have to do more. Much more.

Looking back today, it's all so clear that God was at work throughout, but at the time we felt desperate to change things. It all came to a head when we were involved in two weeks of school mission in Benchill. Back then the area was officially the most deprived in Britain – sitting at the bottom of a list of 34,000 wards in the country. The police didn't like the idea of us hosting an end-of-week gig in the schools, so we booked the local Forum Centre and prayed hard that things wouldn't kick off. In the event the young people loved the gig and were as good as gold, and what was even more exciting was that when I preached the good news at the end, around 100 young people went to the response room to become Christians.

> It was the fulfilment of that prophecy from Isaiah 43 that was given to me years earlier, that 'the wild animals will honour God'

I remember the real sense of God's presence as they repented and did the business with him. Then to cap it all, pretty much all 100 of them turned up for church the following Sunday! Seeing as the church we were partnering with had about twenty members at this point, this really was something of an event! There were the obvious problems that nobody had explained to them – like the fact that you don't bring skateboards and dogs to church – and the few old ladies at the front held tightly to their handbags, but for our part we were absolutely thrilled; to be honest, that Sunday night felt like it was the fulfilment of that prophecy from Isaiah 43 that was given to me years earlier, that *"the wild animals will honour [God], those he has formed to declare his praise"*.

From there on in we did our best to help the local church follow up these young people, but it became obvious that we were all ill-equipped to bring these baby Christians, with all their issues and challenges, to full maturity. Over the next few months we saw most of them fall right back into their old destructive lifestyles. It was absolutely gutting. There had to be a better way than this.

I met up with my friend Frank Green, one of our trustees, and complained about how badly things had gone with these young people. We seemed to have a fantastic model for getting young people to hear the gospel, and we could even get them to make a heartfelt response. But how could we get it to stick?

ABOVE:
OVER THE YEARS THE MESSAGE HAS PRODUCED MANY AWARD-WINNING RESOURCES, SUCH AS GET GOD, FRESH & DEEP. THESE HAVE ALSO BEEN TRANSLATED INTO OTHER LANGUAGES INCLUDING TAJIK, UZBEK, KYRGYZ AND RUSSIAN

BELOW:
MARK SMETHURST AND ANDY TOUR BENCHILL AS THE FIRST EDEN LOCATION

CARL BELCHER PLAYING FOOTBALL WITH A LOCAL YOUTH IN THE EARLY DAYS OF EDEN SALFORD

When I stopped talking, Frank asked me a question. It was simple enough, but it was the point at which our most significant and influential ministry was born.

"What would it take?" he said. I thought for a moment.

"Well for a start, it would take more than us popping in on a Tuesday night to run *Get God* groups. We'd need loads of people living long-term in Benchill as part of the church, plus more prayer, more acts of kindness and lots more resources in the local church."

"Well, why don't we do it? Why not use the platform The World Wide Message Tribe has to recruit modern-day missionaries for Benchill to do just that?"

And so, with Frank's words, the vision for Eden was born. That summer as we did the rounds of the Christian festivals we passionately challenged people to consider moving long-term into Benchill. To our amazement, around three hundred people applied and once we were back home we got about

BELOW:
A HANDFUL OF THE EDEN BENCHILL TEAM

the business of scaling them down. We ended up with 25 amazing people who formed the basis of our new Eden team.

Unfortunately, once we had moved the team in we reverted to type and organised a series of thumping events in the area with loud PA systems, rappers, DJs and preachers. These events invariably ended up with the team going home with black eyes having called the police. It didn't take us long to realise that this approach wasn't working.

It was Laurence Singlehurst who I first heard say "You can't get a ten-tonne truck across a one-tonne bridge." It's true: we can't expect our gospel preaching to truly hit home unless it's being carried across the bridge of relationship. There was possibly no better example of this than our early events in Benchill: the relationships simply weren't ready.

So we stopped the big gigs for a while and our fantastic team focused their efforts on just that – building relationships through detached work, sports, community action and open homes. They backed everything up with lots of prayer, and bit by bit change began to come. Fourteen years later there's still lots of work to do but Benchill is a very different place and I'm convinced that the Eden team and the local churches in partnership played a key part in that.

As we saw this good stuff unfolding it wasn't long before we turned our attention to other deprived estates that were desperately in need of a dose of kingdom life. Things moved fast: as soon as we found partner churches and dedicated people who were called to live this way we rolled out Eden teams around Manchester's toughest estates. Over the next decade 12 more Eden teams were launched and almost 300 people made the sacrificial choice to move into these deprived communities.

Matt Wilson was one of those vital 25 pioneer workers who first showed up in Benchill, and in time he took on the job of leading the fast-growing movement right across the region. In 2008 he came back from holiday convinced that God had spoken: we couldn't keep Eden in Manchester any longer. With just a little bit of tweaking this model that was seeing crime come down, churches grow and communities restored, could work anywhere.

I knew he was right but I did take a bit of convincing. I love Manchester and we'd always been committed to the place. But I knew that this was the right time to lift our eyes and strategically work beyond our beloved city. In time Matt has played a key role in seeing Eden teams launched up and down the country, and today we have more teams outside the M60 than within it.

As I think about the fifteen-year roller coaster that Eden has been on, it's good to remind myself of what happened right at the start. The first time I spoke publicly about the vision was to a group of church leaders in the centre of Manchester. I was encouraged as they prayed for us passionately and we both knew that we had a green light to go ahead.

But that was nothing compared with what happened five minutes after our meeting ended. Simon and I were sat in the car park when a complete stranger came up and knocked on the car window.

RIGHT: MATT WILSON SPEAKING AT THE EDEN AWAY DAY 2010

> **As we saw this good stuff unfolding it wasn't long before we turned our attention to other deprived estates that were desperately in need of a dose of kingdom life**

"I don't know if you are Christians or understand this kind of thing but I believe I've got a word from God for you," he said. "I've been reading my Bible and feel compelled to read these verses to you."

We sat with our chins on the floor as he read Psalm 37:5–11: *"Commit your way to the Lord, trust in him and he will do this: he will make your righteousness shine like the dawn, the justice of your cause like the noonday sun. Be still before the Lord and wait patiently for him; do not fret when men succeed in their ways when they carry out their wicked schemes. Refrain from anger and turn from wrath; do not fret – it leads only to evil. For evil men will be cut off, but those who hope in the Lord will inherit the land. A little while and the wicked will be no more; though you look for them, they will not be found. But the meek will inherit the land and enjoy great peace."*

I truly believe that Almighty God spoke to us on that afternoon in that car park. I believe he told us that the lost, the poor and the hurting on these tough estates are white hot on his heart. I believe that despite the fact that we were heading for good times and bad, the cause of Eden was – and is – a righteous one that would shine brightly. I believe that through it, desert areas will be inherited for Jesus. And you know what? That's exactly what we've seen.

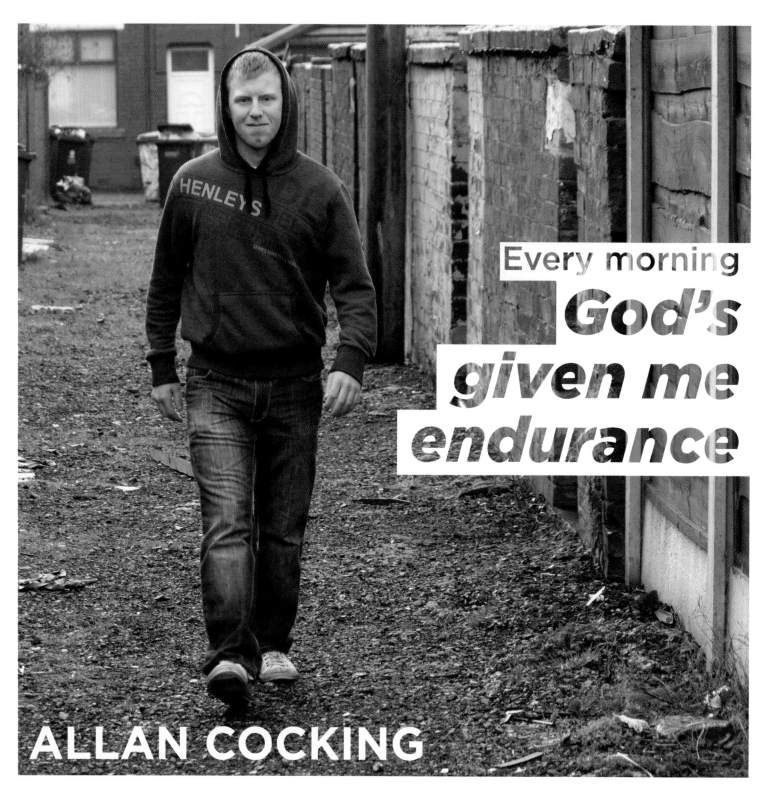

Every morning **God's given me endurance**

ALLAN COCKING

I've got so much to thank God for – he's amazing. Four years ago, I was arrested for robbery, attempting to feed a drug habit that had started with cannabis but had progressed to a £160-a-week cocaine addiction. I escaped a prison sentence but I was given a community service order and had to undergo a drugs treatment course.

Thank God, I met some guys from Eden Westwood and Firwood Church who shared the gospel with me and helped me see how I could start over.

At that point I knew I wanted to be a youth worker. I loved football and playing the guitar in worship and I knew I could be a good role model to lads and help disciple them. So I started a course in Theology at Nazarene College, going back to Oldham to help at Firwood every weekend.

Things were going great: the football ministry was going massively well and we were seeing lots of new faces in our youth work. But things started changing for me.

Around May of 2010, I started noticing weakness in my left hand while I was playing guitar. I went to get physio for a few months but it didn't get any better. As the year went on, the symptoms actually got worse – my walking started to be affected and I was finding it impossible to play the guitar any more.

I was diagnosed this June with motor neurone disease, a condition that affects your nerves and causes weakness and wasting in the muscles. No one knows what causes it and there's no cure – it just gets worse and worse.

People ask me how I'm doing with it and I tell them that I'm up and down with it all the time but my faith is still strong. Every morning God's given me endurance, which I've come to realise is a main part of discipleship. I'm learning that it's OK to admit to problems and struggles and to ask for help. We all need help.

My mobility and dexterity are not what they used to be but for me, the plan has changed, not stopped. I'm going to finish my degree – I passed my first year – although I obviously now need special help writing essays and so on. I still want to do youth work and still can, on a one-to-one relational basis. I'll be doing it, just in different ways and different places.

story 05

GAV HUMPHRIES

totally
TRANSFORMED

> I think part of what makes Eden teams effective at reaching young people is the fact that lots of us can relate to the challenges and temptations they face. We've been there ourselves and we know what it feels like.

I hit a downward spiral from about 13 or 14. My family life wasn't great – I didn't see much of my dad and he never showed much interest in me. So I started getting into trouble. It started with occasional cannabis use but it wasn't long before I was deep into the drugs world, selling drugs around Glossop to support my habit. At 16, I was kicked out of my parents' home and went from dingy flat to friends' floors to living on the streets.

I wasn't someone you could trust anymore. I had a bad reputation and no one wanted to know me. But all I wanted was a relationship with people who cared about me. I got to the point where I was owing thousands of pounds to people, living in a shed, unable to eat or sleep because the drugs had made me paranoid.

Without quite knowing why, I started to yell at God. I didn't even really believe in God, but I didn't know what else to do. I gave him both barrels for three and a half hours – I just told him what I thought of him. By the end I was exhausted. I remember praying, "If you are who you say you are, get me out of this mess!"

And he did – through a random meeting with a lady who looked after me as a kid, I was put in touch with a family who offered me a place to stay – and lots of love.

At one point a group from Canada came to stay who seemed to have something – I didn't know what it was, but I knew I wanted it. They went off to Maidstone in Kent, and I just followed them. While I was there, I gave my life to Christ. Things just clicked. As soon as I said, "Right God, I'm willing to give this a go", my whole demeanour changed. My addiction to drugs was instantly removed. I was totally transformed.

Soon after, God started speaking to me about working with young people, leading to Bible training and opportunities to work in schools and the community. When I first heard about Eden, I knew it was what God had been preparing me for. So in late 2009, my wife Maz and I moved to join Eden Buttershaw, a Bradford estate in the top two percent of deprived wards in England.

God longs for every community to be impacted by his community. I wanted a father – now I've got one. Through Eden, now I'm being a father to others.

story 06

1997

EDEN STARTED IN 1997
IN BENCHILL, WHICH AT THE TIME WAS THE
MOST DEPRIVED COUNCIL WARD IN BRITAIN

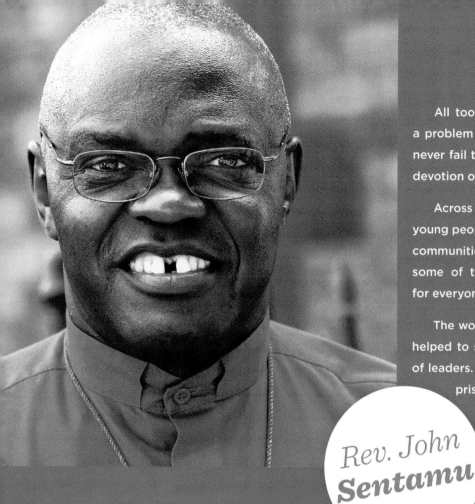

All too often nowadays, society views young people as a problem – in fact young people are part of the solution! I never fail to be inspired by the determination, creativity and devotion of young people.

Across the North of England I have come across so many young people being the change they want to see in their local communities; volunteering their time and energy in making some of the most deprived areas we have better places for everyone.

The work of The Message Trust over the last 20 years has helped to support, encourage and inspire a new generation of leaders. That work goes on through the schools outreach, prison work and myriad other exciting projects.

God calls us to serve others. Put God first, other people second and yourself last. That is the heart of true service.

Never forget the impact small acts of devotion and service can have on the lives of others.

The Message Trust has been touching lives for 20 years, and the journey has only just begun. Here's to the next 20 years!

Rev. John
Sentamu

Congratulations to The Message Trust on 20 years of serving young people in Manchester, and further afield.

THE ARCHBISHOP OF YORK

JULIE MASON

The Eden Bus literally transformed my life

I found my faith at a relatively late stage of my life whilst recovering from a long and debilitating illness. I felt that God was calling me to something but was unsure of what it was.

My local vicar invited me to a meeting in Sharston at somewhere called The Message along with several members from the church. I had a vague notion that it was something to do with kids in the street, and really wasn't interested. But he insisted.

John Robinson was there, talking very movingly about his Eden Bus ministry. I started to feel quite angry: I had no intention of being involved with any teenagers, let alone those who hung around the streets being a pain. In fact, I remember saying angrily "I don't know why I'm even here – I don't do kids". However, through my anger, I clearly heard John say, "...and of course we need someone to learn to drive the bus."

It felt like a bit of a thunderbolt, but I found myself somehow knowing that I had to do this, with my hand up in the air! So off I went and had my bus driving lessons!

story 07

The first project I took the bus out to was a quite an experience. I was absolutely terrified of the kids – they were drunk, swearing and generally unpleasant. But as that night progressed, I found myself chatting away and feeling weirdly comfortable. During the following week, I found myself actually looking forward to the Friday when it was time to do it all again. I was still quite ill at the time, and some weeks I needed to spend most of my time sleeping – but I was happy to sleep all week so that I could take the bus out on the Friday evening – spooky really.

A couple of years later, John called me to tell me that he was leaving the Message and would I be interested in being his replacement? I was totally gobsmacked, but here I am five years later, still loving every minute.

The Eden Bus literally transformed my life. I have come to expect that the fruits of this ministry lie in lost young people being able to find their way, but one of the more surprising joys of my role with Eden Bus is the way it touches the lives of so many volunteers too.

Watching people experiencing a similar growth that I have enjoyed brings about a depth of understanding within their local community and the impact of that can only be positive – I see it as tearing down so many misheld stereotypical opinions.

THE BOY WHO BECAME A MAN

has had a great impact on many lives.

BY SAM WARD:
EDEN OPENSHAW

IN MEMORY OF
CODY O'GRADY

I first met Cody when he was nine or ten. He and a group of friends wanted to come into our youth club but they were just too young – although it wasn't long before he made the leap to secondary school and was welcomed as a regular.

Cody was a popular kid, liked by both leaders and peers. He could lark around with the best of them; Cody is responsible for the bog roll balls that to this day remain firmly fixed to the ceiling of the male toilet and after six years they cling on almost as a papier-mâché symbol of defiance. I can remember the endless times I would find him hiding beneath the pool table and would have to peel him from his mates who clung to him like life depended on it all in the vain hope of being able to remain in the youth club once the doors had shut and everyone else had gone home. The youth club was his own and he would have stayed all night if we'd let him.

Cody also had an incredibly tender side that meant he would be happy to sit and talk to you about life, the universe and everything, asking questions and sharing thoughts about the deepest of things while the chaos of youth club rumbled on around him. Our relationship intensified when he became the innocent victim of a hit-and-run accident as Cody walked to our club one Thursday evening. I had the job of telling his parents and taking them to the hospital to visit him. He made a full recovery but little did I know of the many more hospital visits that were to come.

It was at our Wednesday night football session that I first noticed the swelling around his eye. Cody's nose was blocked too so his doctor had said he had a sinus infection which would pass with antibiotics. At youth club the next week it was clear for all that this was no sinus infection. Cody's eye was now bulging from the side of his face; he was embarrassed and confused about what was happening to him. I took him out into the small room at the back of our hall, where he told me that the doctors had said they thought he had cancer and they had referred him to The Christie for further investigation.

I got a call a couple of days later at 2.30am in the morning from Cody's dad, Steve. He said Cody was in a bad way so I rushed straight round. When we arrived, Cody was struggling to move and could hardly breathe. We rushed him to Christie's who told us that the tumour was growing at an alarming rate and was cutting off his wind pipe and beginning to surround his brain. They started chemotherapy that night. Within days I was flying off on holiday and thought that there was every chance that Cody would die while I was away. As soon as we touched down at Manchester Airport, I phoned to find out the news. The chemo had worked, Cody was well, sat up and waiting to see me.

There was still plenty of work to do. Cody was diagnosed with rhabdomyosarcoma, a rare form of soft tissue cancer, so numerous rounds of chemotherapy and radiotherapy were in order. The treatment put him in incredible pain – he seemed to suffer with every side effect and eating was excruciating. A skinny kid when healthy, it was shocking to see him lose weight so fast. Cody also had to overcome his claustrophobia as he spent many hours in scanning and radiotherapy machines.

Cody was battling hard and was winning, doctors reported that the tumour had responded to the treatment and was all but gone.

I wanted to recognise Cody's heroic fight so nominated him for an Urban Hero Award for courage and it was no surprise that he won. But as the awards night approached, things very unexpectedly took a turn for the worse. Cody suffered two significant attacks, like strokes, that left him comatose for days.

At first doctors thought this was simply a reaction to his many months of treatment but tests revealed that Cody's cancer had reappeared in the lining around his brain.

As he lay comatose for the second time, doctors said he would not make it through the night and the family were called to pay their final respects. But the unexpected happened: Cody bounced back again, and by the morning he was awake and wondering what all the fuss was about. Doctors extended his life expectancy from a couple of hours to a couple of months and admitted there was nothing further they could do.

With only a handful of people knowing the prognosis, Cody stood strong in front of the many hundreds of guests at the Urban Hero Awards Ceremony. We all celebrated his fight, yet knew that the hardest fight was still to come. His courage was clear for all to see. Cody fought on, living each day at a time.

A rapid decline saw Cody readmitted to hospital in late August but he requested to be allowed home. Doctors granted his last wish and Cody passed away peacefully in his own bed on September 8th, 2010.

His memory lives on as we continue to serve young people like Cody in our neighbourhood. The boy who became a man has had a great impact on many lives. I know mine will never be the same again.

There is a beautiful legacy that lives on with the passing of Cody O'Grady. The change in Cody's parents Steve and Debbie has been remarkable. Both have been long-term heroin addicts; Steve admits he has probably smoked over half a million pounds worth of drugs in his life and I imagine Debbie wasn't too far behind. Cody's illness heaped additional pressure on to already strained lives as each day they tried to manage the chaotic lifestyle of addiction with caring for their son. A constant bedside vigil gave them lots of time to reflect and evaluate and many promises were made about how life should change.

I think the turning point was the moment when Cody was given morphine to relieve his suffering. He had been fearful of taking pain relief as he was concerned he would become an addict like his parents. Morphine is a derivative of the opium poppy from which the heroin they were so dependent on is made. As Cody resigned himself to accepting the drugs, they vowed to reject it and seek help. From the day after Cody's funeral they asked me to contact the community drugs team and help them start the process of withdrawal. Debbie and Steve have continued to be a part of our lives. For many weeks they would come to youth club and helped out. Supporting what their son loved has become very important to them. So far they have organised two events to raise money to help us buy the piece of land next to our building so that our work can be improved and expanded.

They seem to enjoy being around us and the feeling are reciprocated. I am not sure if they have joined our family or whether we have joined theirs, but they come and see me and the team every day and sit and chat about life, the universe and everything. Debbie recently cooked me a Sunday roast which would rival any Christmas feast. The hardness has mellowed and there is a fresh attitude of thanksgiving and generosity. I sense there is a new hope and the future is no longer something to be feared. Their friendship is so precious and I thank God for their lives.

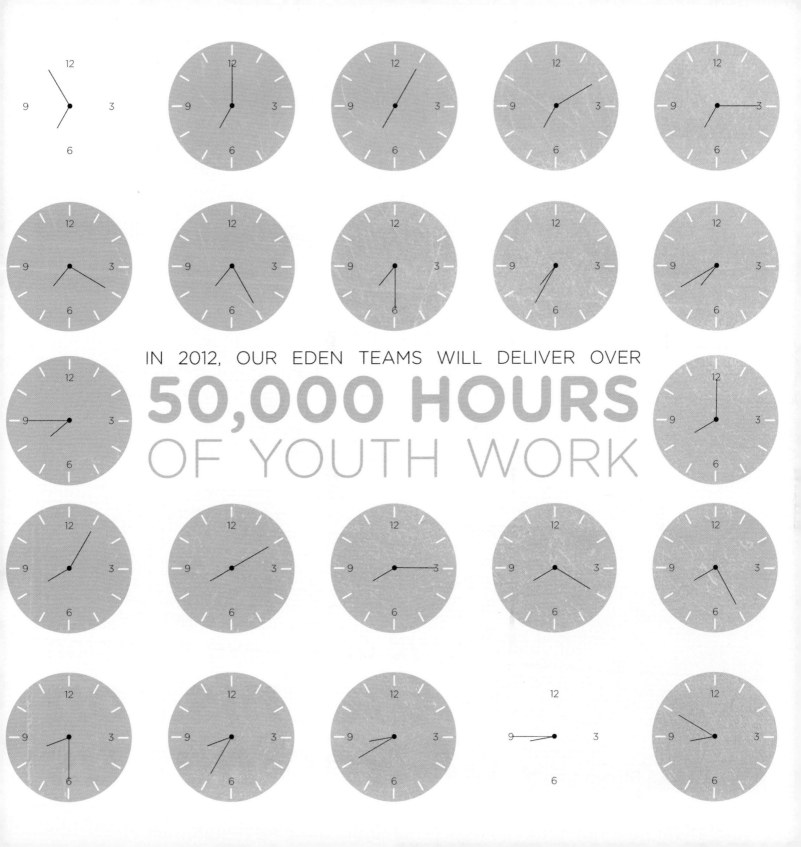

IN 2012, OUR EDEN TEAMS WILL DELIVER OVER
50,000 HOURS
OF YOUTH WORK

SID WILLIAMS

We don't have a mission
*- the mission
of God has us*

I first encountered the Message when I was 15, joining in the Message 2000 city mission and being wrongly allocated to a youth project in the streets of Moss Side despite having asked to do a 'safe' cafe outreach! I loved it and remember growing in my desire for mission.

Even then I wondered if I would be adventurous enough to join an Eden project if I had been old enough. At the age of 18 God showed me his heart for justice, giving me a vision of deprived young people, the homeless and people in prostitution. My ambition to become a graphic designer was cut short and swapped for a much bigger adventure. I asked God whether I should do the Xcelerate course and he answered in an astonishing way that I don't have space to explain here!

The course really spurred me on in my faith and provided me with a clear calling to Eden in Harpurhey. After nine months back down South working with excluded young people and setting up a youth church event, I joined the Eden team and also made it a placement for a youth work degree. My calling developed initially through youth work and praying for the sick on the estates and on to public preaching. It was great to be surrounded by people so keen to change a community.

At times our commitment to families led us to have children live with us to help families cope, and taught me a fair amount about being a parent to teenagers! After a few years I decided to tackle unemployment by taking young men to work in construction and God provided some fantastic work for us to carry out and train lads in. I worked with six young men for two and a half years and had to trust God for his provision. And together with a friend we took six young men to Kenya to build a school in a slum there. It was an amazing project and we are now involved long-term with five schools there. Each time, God provided amazingly though it was tough.

Today, I'm still in Harpurhey, now working for Christ Church. Seven years isn't that long really, and it feels like I'm just getting started. Together, we're chasing God and expecting to see hundreds of young people and their families come to know Jesus. We don't have a mission – the mission of God has us.

The best is yet to come!

NATASHA POLLITT

I'll always remember the people **who helped me**

When the Eden team came to where I lived in Hattersley, I was 14. I had what some people would call a 'chaotic' home life but the truth was a lot worse than that. I had been abused emotionally and physically by this time and I was drinking and doing drugs a lot to hide the pain. I look back now and realise I had no dreams and I basically hated my life.

The Eden project was the start of a journey for me which had a lot of positives even if there were some negatives. My mindset began to change as I was surrounded by people who really cared about me, and a sense of family and belonging. I'll always remember the people who helped me: Sharon and John Murphy were especially amazing, and John and Sam Patterson and many others helped me through. It was the beginning of my relationship with God and the start of my healing.

I remember being invited to London to share my testimony and thinking about how far I'd come from where I had been. I noticed how much I had changed and yet I knew there was still lots of pain that hadn't been dealt with.

In time, I had the feeling it was time to get away from Manchester. I had a feeling I should be helping other young people in the same situation as I had been in to show them that there was a different way of life. So I signed up to join a new Eden team in Sheffield.

It was a big breakthrough for me and quite quickly we were doing things in the community with the church, meeting people, setting up girls' groups and running Christian discipleship activities.

story 10

During this time, God brought up a lot of things in me. I started to realise things about my life that needed dealing with. I needed serious help and I found it in a church-based rehabilitation programme called City Hearts.

I left City Hearts in June 2011 and I'm feeling great. God's done a work in me and it feels like a new beginning.

CHAPTER FOUR

Making Music, Changing Lives

**WORLD WIDE MESSAGE TRIBE:
TAKE A LONG HIKE**
RELEASED: 1993

**WORLD WIDE MESSAGE TRIBE:
DANCE PLANET**
RELEASED: 1994

**PLANET LIFE
STARTS IN ST MARY'S
CHEADLE**

**MOVATION FEATURING WWMT:
JUMPING IN THE HOUSE OF GOD**
RELEASED: 1995

**WORLD WIDE MESSAGE TRIBE:
WE DON'T GET WHAT WE DESERVE**
RELEASED: 1995

**MOVATION FEATURING WWMT:
JUMPING IN THE HOUSE OF GOD II**
RELEASED: 1996

**WORLD WIDE MESSAGE TRIBE:
REVIVED**
RELEASED: 1996

**WWMT COLLECTED
4 GMA AWARDS
INCLUDING 3 DOVE
AWARDS**

**WORLD WIDE MESSAGE TRIBE:
HEATSEEKER**
RELEASED: 1997

**ANDY 'THE
HEAVYFOOT'
HAWTHORNE HANGS
UP HIS BOOTS**

**MOVATION:
JUMPING IN THE HOUSE OF GOD III**
RELEASED: 1998

**WWMT
FRANTIK ALBUM & SINGLE**
RELEASED: 1999

PLANET LIFE: LIVE & LARGE
RELEASED: 2000

**NAME OFFICIALLY
CHANGED TO JUST,
THE TRIBE**

**THE TRIBE:
TAKE BACK THE BEAT
ALBUM & SINGLE**
RELEASED: 2001

**THE TRIBE:
RAISE YOUR GAME ALBUM
& B-BOY SINGLE**
RELEASED: 2003

**IT ALL STARTED WITH THIS CASSETTE TAPE
WWMT: TAKE A LONG HIKE**
RELEASED: 1992

What started with Mark Pennells and his solo pop songs has grown and grown over the years. We have found so many artists who all carry the same passion for reaching young people, and while the sounds have changed, the hearts have all beat to the sound of the same drum.

Our girl band, Blush^UK, hit on a particularly fruitful ministry helping other young women discover their true worth, and this work is now being carried on through an all-new girls' ministry, RUBYGIRL UK.

We've also played a part in releasing the hard-hitting theatre company In Yer Face. I think it's true to say that in the UK, Christian theatre is often slightly cheesy and embarrassing. But you could never say that about In Yer Face. They travel around schools and prisons and always make a massive impression. And it's also been a delight to see Twelve24 grow and thrive. It's made up of former Genetik students Josh, Ryan and Christina, who together are now reaching many young people in the schools of Manchester.

Perhaps our best known band since The World Wide Message Tribe are LZ7. They were formed by Lindsay West who has proved to be one of the UK's most effective evangelists. Each week at LZ7 concerts and schools weeks, literally hundreds of young people are giving their lives to Christ. In 2009 the band recorded a song called *This Little Light* as a bit of an afterthought on their *Gasoline* album. But there was something about the song, and due to the buzz that followed it, the band decided to spend a day in a local high school producing a video with the young people to accompany it.

**BLUSH UK:
YOU GOT NOTHING ON ME**
RELEASED: 2003

**BLUSH UK:
SUNSHINE**
RELEASED: 2004

**WWMT/THE TRIBE
TAKE THEIR
FINAL BOW AT
THE MANCHESTER
APOLLO DEC '04**

**THE TRIBE:
MESSAGE TO THE MASSES**
RELEASED: 2004

**LZ7:
RUCKUS**
RELEASED: 2005

**BREATHE WAS
THE 1ST FULL
WORSHIP ALBUM**

**ANDY SMITH:
BREATHE**
RELEASED: 2007

**EAR CANDY
NOMINATED
FOR A MOBO
MUSIC AWARD**

**BLUSH UK:
EAR CANDY**
RELEASED: 2007

**LZ7:
GASOLINE**
RELEASED: 2008

**TWELVE24:
TWELVE24**
RELEASED: 2009

**BLUSH UK:
BEAUTIFUL (SINGLE)**
RELEASED: 2009

**THIS LITTLE
LIGHT REACHED
No. 26 IN THE
UK CHARTS**

**LZ7:
THIS LITTLE LIGHT (SINGLE)**
RELEASED: 2010

**LZ7:
LIGHT**
RELEASED: 2010

**TWELVE24:
BETTER WORDS**
RELEASED: 2011

IN YER FACE THEATRE COMPANY

BLUSH UK ON STAGE AND IN SCHOOL

The video was posted on YouTube and very quickly had over 100,000 views and lots of great comments from young people saying how much the song meant to them. People posted great stories of coming to Christ through the band's work, and the buzz got even louder. We realised we were really on to something when LZ7's record label suggested we release the song into the mainstream, with EMI getting on board with distribution and marketing. The song was duly released and reached a high of number 26 in the UK singles chart – as far as we know the highest ever placing by an overtly evangelistic band. So many good things have come out of this – not least a hugely increased profile for the band and thus lots more young people at their gigs. And then there's the wonderful Shine Your Light movement which has encouraged thousands of young people to share their faith and engage in multiple acts of kindness.

ABI SEWART

The Tribe came into my school
and they changed my life
FOREVER

Back in September 2003 when I was 12 years old, a crazy bunch of Christians came into my school, calling themselves The Tribe. They came into my school at a crucial time in my life – a few months earlier, in April 2003, my dad had suddenly died and I was dealing with the grief in a bad way.

The Tribe came into my school and they changed my life forever. They changed my view of Christians and I became a Christian at the end of week gig. The story didn't end there though – I never stopped following The Tribe as well as Blush[UK], LZ7 and Twelve24. Even to this day I am a massive fan and proud of it.

In 2004 when the Tribe ended I remember being given a flyer about a training programme called Genetik. Even then I knew that this was what I wanted to do when I was old enough. Being 16 years old I was still too young so I started to do Genetik Sessions to see what it was all about. This was where I found my passion for singing... and then I found I couldn't stop singing!

Finally, at the age of 19, I got a place on Genetik. This was where the real transformation happened. I joined Genetik in 2010 as a girl who had self-esteem problems, who wasn't really fully on fire for

story 11

God and just wanted to sing but didn't have that much confidence in myself.

After an incredible year I finished Genetik in 2011 as a confident, beautiful, fully-on-fire-for-God, passionate young lady. Amazingly, I have even been offered the opportunity to start going into schools doing self-esteem courses for girls with RUBYGIRL UK!

God totally transformed me and showed me who I was in his eyes – that he thinks I am beautiful just the way I am and that's all that really matters. I want to thank The Message Trust for all the support that you have given me over the years. You guys are truly AMAZING! I love you all so much!

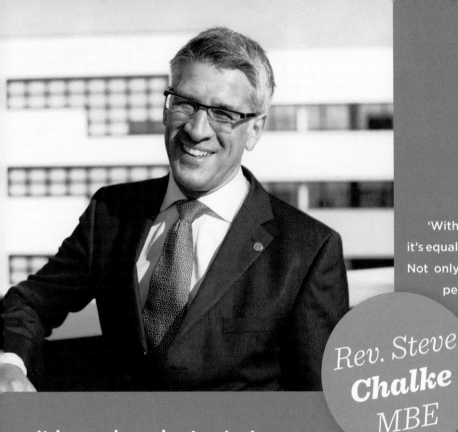

Rev. Steve Chalke MBE

'Without a vision the people perish', the Bible teaches. But it's equally true that 'without management the vision perishes'. Not only is Andy Hawthorne an exceptional visionary who perseveres for the long haul, but within The Message Trust he has been, and remains, surrounded by countless other deeply committed individuals and a team of outstanding leaders.

Over these twenty years literally tens of thousands of individuals have been transformed as they have discovered Christ through the work of The Message Trust. And it's not just been the young, but countless people of all ages who through their involvement have encountered Jesus on a deeper and more profound level.

But here's the biggest thing: across the years, The Message has inspired hundreds of other groups to dare to dream and then to deliver their own projects and programmes. The impact that The Message has had, and will continue to have, both in the UK and around the world, simply can't be measured.

Here's to the next twenty years!

It is much easier to start something than to sustain it. So the fact that after twenty years The Message Trust is still growing, adventuring and pioneering is a masterclass in vision, creativity, energy, focus, commitment, hard work and resilience.

FOUNDER OF OASIS TRUST

MEG HOWARD

I found
my voice

In 1999 I went to a Tribe concert in Essex which literally changed my life. The Tribe spoke about Jesus in a way that I had never heard before and challenged all my preconceived ideas about faith.

I gave my life to God that night and prayed a prayer with all of my heart – I told God that if there was one thing I'd like to achieve with my life it would be to follow in The Tribe's footsteps and introduce young people to Jesus, just like they had done for me.

I remember telling God that I had absolutely no idea how he was going to do it, because I seriously struggled with my confidence, but that I would trust Him to direct my path. Throughout my teens, especially as friends were making university plans, I became increasingly excited to see what God would do with my life.

Through an amazing turn of events, I heard about an audition up in Manchester for a girl band called tbc. When I read that the audition was to be at The Message building I think I had heart palpitations!

Still to this day I don't know how I didn't faint with nerves! I was a quivering wreck.

The day I got the call to say I had been accepted, I was simply overwhelmed. Innervation had given the job to a shy, nervous 19-year old who cried at the drop of a hat! How did that happen? It felt like a miracle – God had listened to my dream seven years before and I was on my way.

I moved to Manchester in 2006 and spent three and a half years in the band. It was the most incredible time, meeting some fantastic people and working alongside some of my heroes. A huge transformation happened in me throughout tbc as I found my voice and was able to share the good news with around 250,000 young people across the world!

story 12

I left tbc in 2010 and now head up an initiative called KOKO – a new online community for girls launching in 2012. Our heart is to support, encourage and inspire girls around the world as well as creatively communicate the gospel with them.

The Message ignited a flame in my life and now I'm bursting with passion for Jesus and to see young people around the world come to know him.

BETH STOUT

I developed a huge heart for working with teenage girls

story 13

Growing up in Liverpool in the late 1990s and early 2000s, I can remember queuing at Tribe concerts many, many times!

**BELOW:
BETH AND GOLDDIGGER
BANDMATE MANDY**

I was about 14 when I first heard about Xcelerate at Soul Survivor one year and had an overwhelming feeling that I had to go on the course when I left school, yet had a nagging feeling that God wanted me to use my skills in performing arts, and so debated with God if Manchester was really the place for me. I remember praying about it and really clearly hearing God say, 'Leave it with me, Beth – I'll sort it.' And he did – by the year I finished my A Levels, Xcelerate became Genetik and there was a creative arts stream. Right away I knew God had been guiding me there all along!

I was part of the Genetik course in 2006, and it completely changed my life. The teaching, training and support really encouraged me to grow in my gifts, but mainly challenged me to work on my character, becoming the person God had created me to be. My leaders stretched me to be the very best, both as a performer and as a follower of Jesus.

My time on Genetik was so foundational for what God had in store for me next. Whilst I was on the course, I developed a huge heart for working with teenage girls and for creative arts but was never sure how they could fit together. After Genetik, I worked for Reflex in prisons and then went back to Liverpool to be youth pastor for a local church, always feeling like God had more in store.

And then three years ago, God called me to move to Sheffield to help run a Christian youth work charity called GoldDigger Trust, working with young girls on issues of self-esteem, self harm, eating disorders and sexual relationships. We run courses with girls in schools and youth centres, and recently opened a centre in the heart of Sheffield working with teenage girls who are being sexually exploited.

As well as this, we do schools work and gigs across the UK with the GoldDigger band. My training from Genetik, plus ongoing support from The Message has really helped me and GoldDigger to be excellent in what we do – one of the values that really sticks out to me from Genetik and my time with The Message. And we still keep in touch, from gigging alongside LZ7 to coming back to teach on the new Genetik course, it has been a huge privilege to be able to input into the next generation of creative evangelists and youth workers and pass on what people invested into me back then.

CHAPTER FIVE

Words and Actions... the Perfect Partnership

1996 was a busy year but we found time to get The World Wide Message Tribe over to Dresden, Germany to be involved in something called Christival. This was a huge city-wide festival with 13 stages rammed full with a variety of evangelistic events. The irrepressible Roland Werner had a vision of 10,000 young people on the streets witnessing for Christ and bringing people along to the evening meetings. They ended up getting 35,000 involved and turned another 20,000 away! Thousands of young people came to Christ through Christival and it was a privilege to be involved.

We came back feeling determined to try and do something similar in Manchester in the millennium year, but it was only a few months later – when we shared a fateful cup of coffee with Mike Pilavachi – that the plans took off into orbit. We'd been telling Mike about Christival as well as Eden and our own vision for Manchester and he seemed to get really fired up. A few days later he phoned me with the craziest of ideas: why not cancel Soul Survivor in the year 2000 and move his 20,000 punters lock, stock, and barrel to Manchester to serve, Christival style?

Obviously I was excited but as we started to plan, Mike threw in a bit of a curve ball – one that has actually changed the way we and lots of other people have done their mission ever since. He said he thought that at least 40% of the delegates should be involved in servant outreach and community action – removing rubbish and graffiti, painting houses,

> If they were going to start praising our Father in heaven then they needed to see our faith in action

ON THE STAGE: THE VAST CROWDS AT F:M 2003

ON THE STREETS: BIG DEAL COMMUNITY
ACTION PROJECT 2008

cleaning cars and so on. At first my evangelical hackles rose and I thought "what has washing cars and painting houses got to do with the gospel?" But as I thought and prayed about it, it struck me that maybe the people of Manchester did need to see our good deeds a bit more. If they were going to start praising our Father in heaven then maybe they did need to see our faith in action. Plus there was the small fact that Mike, the Pied Piper of Soul Survivor, was actually recruiting the vast majority of young people.

In the year-long build-up to Soul Survivor – Message 2000 we saw around 500 local missions take place, and when the many thousands of young people arrived and camped at Heaton Park there were hundreds of projects going on all over the city for them to get involved with. In the evening we held huge evangelistic gigs at the Manchester Evening News Arena and once again, thousands came to know Christ. To be honest it was a huge headache to pull it all off but God brought an amazing team together; the budget was once again raised by the skin of our teeth and all in all it was massively worth it, particularly as so many of the young people involved

ABOVE:
A DELEGATE AT
FESTIVAL
MANCHESTER
TALKING WITH
A LOCAL YOUNG
PERSON

took the model back to their home churches and started to deliver 'word and deed' mission week in and week out.

One unforgettable highlight of Message 2000 was the Swinton Valley Project. The Valley was a notorious crime black spot known locally as The Bronx, but a Christian police officer, Phil Gleave, offered to oversee a team of a thousand young people who would spend ten days blitzing the area with love and kindness. During this time something amazing happened to the place as local residents joined in with Christian young people to totally clean up the estate, creating a community garden as well as a dog walking track and refurbishing the run-down community and resource centres. By the end all I can say is that you could feel a tangible sense of the presence of God throughout the area. Amazingly there wasn't one recorded incident of crime in the place for the whole ten days, and following the mission there was an almost 50% reduction in crime. Rather than rows of boarded-up houses, people began queuing up to move into an area that had had such a massive dose of God's goodness.

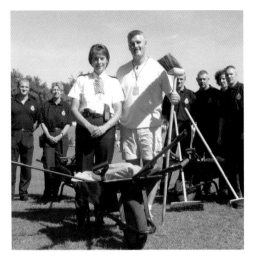

Once the dust had settled and all the bills had been paid I was keen to do something big again. So I didn't take much convincing when the Luis Palau Association contacted us to see if we would partner in a huge open-air festival that they wanted to bring to Manchester. I went over to the States to see their new model in action – it involved great bands and entertainment, a kids' area, skate park, fun fair and all the rest. And right at the centre of it all was a clear presentation of the good news of Jesus and an opportunity to respond. I loved it but my only proviso if we were going to get involved was that we recruited thousands of young people to work on the streets and – guess what – that at least 40% of them were involved in community action projects. I could almost feel the hardcore evangelist Luis Palau's eyebrows raising, but his team agreed to it all and brought plenty of wisdom, resources and faith to help pull off our biggest initiative to date. Festival:Manchester again saw hundreds of local projects impact the community and 65,000 people show up for the main event. Interestingly the Luis Palau Association now almost always involves young people in random acts of kindness when they host their mega-festivals around the world.

On the back of all this, other cities got in on the action and we were involved at various levels in events like Merseyfest, NE1 in the North East and the biggest of the lot, Soul In The City in the capital. I'm sure that these events became the catalyst for church leaders across the country to think much more seriously about community engagement, and these days it's unusual to meet a leader who just wants to focus on their own church meetings rather than get out there and impact society.

> " Festival:Manchester again saw hundreds of local projects impact the community and 65,000 people show up for the main event "

After Soul In The City in 2005 I met up again with my friends Mike Pilavachi and Roy Crowne (who was heading up Youth for Christ). There were other opportunities to work in other cities, but we felt this wasn't the way forward. Perhaps instead we could get the whole church – right across the UK – to spend an entire year getting out and serving their communities with word and action? After lots of conversations with key leaders we decided to go for it and to call it Hope '08. We set ourselves the goal of seeing 500 areas up and down the country working together across the denominations to offer creative, servant-hearted mission. In the end we saw almost 1,500 regions take part and thousands of local initiatives make a difference.

It felt like a God thing and I'm really pleased that recently Roy Crowne has moved over from Youth for Christ to head up Hope Together with plans to have another go at blitzing the nation with kindness and unashamed proclamation in 2014.

I love what Pete Greig has said about The Message in his kind piece in this book. He's been doing his best to cheer us on over the last twenty years because of the way we 'combine social justice with courageous proclamation of the gospel.' I've become convinced that this is the only way to get the job done and that one without the other is only half a gospel. As we move forward, our job is to make sure we keep working hard on both fronts.

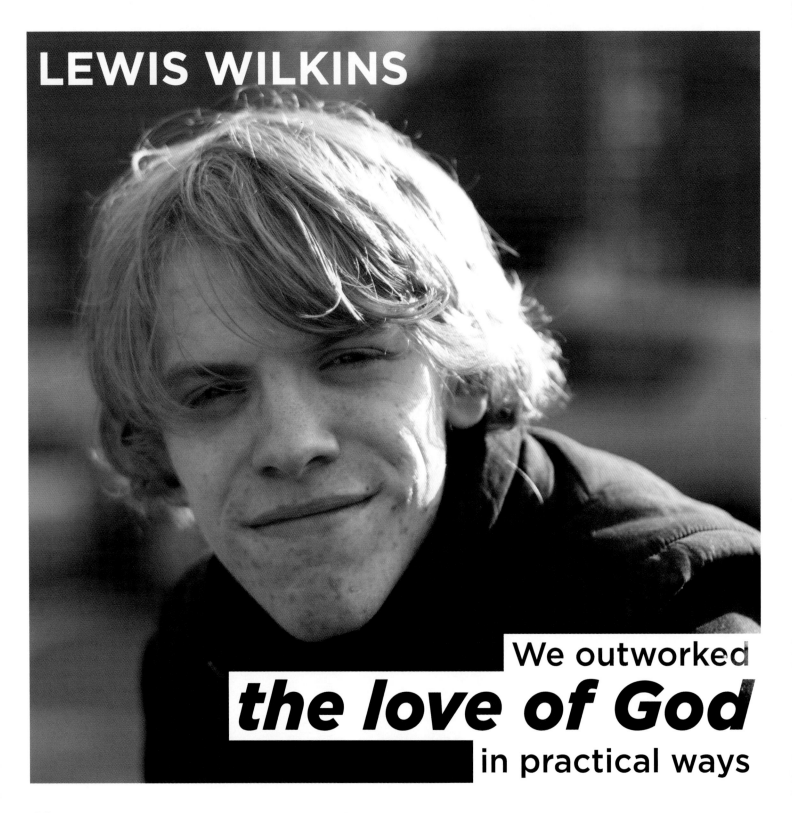

LEWIS WILKINS

We outworked **the love of God** in practical ways

For me it all started at Message 2000, an evangelistic event held at the MEN Arena and on community action projects in different places around the city. I was 8 years old and I came to the event with my mum. I was very young but I clearly remember that was where I made the decision to live for Christ... that was my first encounter with The Message Trust.

A few years later I was involved again, this time getting my hands dirty as part of Festival:Manchester. We outworked the love of God in practical ways by doing various things like litter picking and cleaning people's gardens around my local estate.

The next time I came across The Message was a few years later when I was a bit older. It was an event called Urban Adventure, based at !Audacious City Church. This was where my life took a big turn for the better.

Urban Adventure was an incredible missions week, with the gospel preached through gigs and on social action projects in the ten boroughs of Greater Manchester. There were street clean-ups, painting railings, car washes, barbecues, children's activities, fun day, youth concerts – loads of things run by churches to bring communities together and share about Jesus.

I was shoved right out of my comfort zone, not only because of the practical work but because it was the first time I had ever prayed out loud in a group of people, and I prayed for none other than the founder of The Message Trust, Andy Hawthorne! Talk about thrown into the deep end!

But the story didn't end there. After Urban Adventure I started going along to !Audacious City Church on and off for a few months until I made the decision to make it my home church. Since then I have been involved in !Audacious Church creative team and have learned so many priceless skills and lessons. Now I am on the !Audacious Academy with an unbelievable year ahead. It would be safe to say without The Message Trust I would not be where I am today.

story 14

LEWIS (FAR RIGHT) WITH OTHER YOUNG PEOPLE AT THE URBAN ADVENTURE

Mike
Pilavachi

In 1998 I met Andy for coffee at Spring Harvest. I expected that we would ask each other how things were going in our respective ministries and listen politely as we took it in turns to tell each other the 'Holy Ghost stories'. I asked Andy how he was doing and listened. And listened. And listened. I never got the chance to tell my stories! Andy launched passionately into a very long monologue about his desire to give every young person in Manchester an opportunity to hear the gospel. He also told me in detail how he was going to do it. By the end of the coffee I had committed Soul Survivor to cancel our summer events in 2000 and instead bring thousands of young people to Manchester to help The Message with their mission. It nearly killed us but it was the best decision we ever made. We had an amazing time that summer and it has changed the course of our ministry ever since.

I first met Andy Hawthorne when the World Wide Message Tribe played a gig at a Soul Survivor conference in 1996. I was mesmerised. They were professional, brilliantly produced and well choreographed. And yet that wasn't what caught my attention. There was something more. This was pure, raw, passionate evangelism.

I loved it and felt such a sense of relief. The more I got to know Andy the more I caught his passion for reaching the lost and seeing revival. The Message as an organisation and a movement both reflects and expresses Andy's passion. They are single-minded. They are determined. They know what they are for and they give themselves wholeheartedly to their calling. They seek and serve the lost and the disadvantaged, in Manchester and throughout the UK. Over the years they have remained faithful to their core mission and have resisted all the temptations to divert from the path.

Years later and Andy is still at it. His passion has not wavered and the zeal is as fervent as ever. So what are the lessons we can all learn from The Message? First, go to God for your marching orders and then stay stubbornly faithful to those orders. Secondly, persevere. Keep going, on good days and bad days. Thirdly, love, honour and serve the whole church. Fourthly, be transparently and overwhelmingly pushy about the ministry you passionately believe in. Fifthly, pray! Prayer has been the engine room that has driven all that The Message have done over the years.

Andy is a wonderful friend and a faithful provoker and The Message is greatly admired by all of us at Soul Survivor. I am incredibly thankful for all the Lord has taught us through them but most of all, for everything they have done for the kingdom of God.

FOUNDER AND LEADER OF SOUL SURVIVOR

Since Message 2000,
young people on our teams have delivered
500,000 hours
of community action
in Greater Manchester
at a value of over £3m

£3 million

building bridges & trust

between the young and old

PAUL & TINA HUXLEY

Message 2000 was a kick-start for several new churches and community organisations, including ours: G-Force, a charity working with children, young people and families on the Broomwood estate in South Trafford.

At the time we were leading a Christian youth group and the four days of social action activities during Message 2000 helped to highlight the needs in Broomwood for us.

For Message 2000, we had 100 volunteers come into the area to do projects focusing on cleaning up the woods, shifting rubbish, planting flower beds and cleaning round the youth centre and getting to know local kids, with a big fun day to close. There were big issues on the estate which we knew were there but this really brought them into the light.

It seemed natural for us to set up a community association, involving parents and local residents. This led to God opening doors up for us supporting needy individuals and families; special courses in local schools; adult education classes and groups for the elderly; an arts and crafts drop-in in Altrincham town centre.

We also opened a community cafe in the heart of the Broomwood that hosts a credit union, benefits and job advice drop-ins as well as debt counselling. G-Force was also the lead agency involved in the revamping of the local park, drawing in over £150k worth of funding to make it happen.

Over the last 12 years, the work has won several awards, and we have attracted funding from local authorities and businesses. What started as a small youth group surviving on revenues from the tuck-shop on a Saturday night has now become a registered charity employing five full-time staff and a host of part-time workers in regular contact with over 700 children and young people a year. The inter-generational aspect of the work G-Force now does also helped to build bridges and trust between the young and old making the community feel better about itself.

For us, there were several key milestones in the development of G-Force and one of those was Message 2000 and all those guys coming in. The impression they made and the impact within the hearts of the people in the community was huge – they didn't just change the environment but there was a sea-change in the way local people looked at their community. They saw how it could change and the assets that were there but were being overlooked and how they could make that change happen. It was as if they suddenly realised, 'Hey, we can do stuff here!'

All this was built on a foundation inspired by the practical work of Message 2000.

story 15

CHAPTER SIX

Never Forget...

Early on in 2001, in the aftermath of Message 2000, I arrived back in the office after a few days' break. Claire, my secretary at the time, said there was a prophetess from Dallas who wanted to come and bring me 'the word of the Lord' with me and my wife Michele. "No chance," I thought, but then fortunately changed my mind. "But make sure she has only got thirty minutes," I said to Claire. I rang Michele and she agreed to join us at the office.

ANDY AND MICHELE HAWTHORNE WITH COMPASSION SPONSORED KIDS, HAITI

> **Through child sponsorship, various events and offerings and through our tithe account at The Message we have been able to see hundreds of thousands raised for this work in Haiti**

The lady came in and all my fears were confirmed. She looked like a typical televangelist's wife and said everything in a loud voice.

"I've made sure I know nothing about you, but the Lord has spoken," she said, before turning to Michele. "The Lord has seen your heart for the hurting women and now he says he is ready to open doors so you can bless these women."

She was bang on, so Michele started crying and the presence of God was clearly in the room. Then she turned to me and said, "The Lord has seen your heart for urban youth and he's pleased with this, but today he says never forget the poorest of the poor."

I knew it was God but wasn't sure what to do about it until a couple of days later. My friend Ian Hamilton – who used to be an executive at our record company – phoned and invited me to visit Haiti with him to see the work of Compassion, the amazing child sponsorship charity. I'm not sure if I would have taken him up on this offer if it hadn't been for the 'word' from the American prophetess, but I'm so glad I did. Over the last decade the work of Compassion – particularly the wonderful things they do in Haiti – has really got under our skin.

Now, every time we take on a member of staff we sponsor a child in Haiti. We've encouraged our supporters to help support Compassion and together they've sponsored hundreds more. We've been involved in water projects, orphanages and the rebuilding of a hospital that was damaged during the 2010 earthquake.

Through child sponsorship, various events and offerings and through our tithe account at The Message we have been able to see hundreds of thousands of pounds raised for this work in Haiti. But as is always the case when you give to the poorest of the poor, we've received so much more back. I've been able to go back to Haiti six times since, including a totally traumatic and unforgettable visit with medical supplies and food a few days after the cataclysmic earthquake. But even then nothing quite beats the sight of a healthy, happy beautiful young Haitian Christian who you witnessed on a previous visit fighting for survival but who now, through the work of Compassion, has been saved in every possible way. There's really nothing better.

1	2	3
4	5	6
7	8	9

1,4,6) MEMBERS OF BLUSH UK IN HAITI. THEIR TRACK 'NOT ALONE' WAS INSPIRED BY THEIR EXPERIENCES

2) MESSAGE STAFF MEMBER STEVE OLDHAM IN UGANDA WITH ACT4AFRICA

3) JUSTIN DOWDS FROM LEMON AID WHO WE HAVE WORKED WITH IN HAITI DELIVERING AID AND CLEAN WATER SUPPLIES

5,9) SHOTS TAKEN DURING OUR RECENT TRIPS TO HAITI

7) LINDZ WEST CHASES AFTER A LOCAL BUS

8) ANDY'S BROTHER SIMON CAUGHT THE SAME HEART FOR THE POOREST OF THE POOR AND NOW WORKS WITH DALIT CHILDREN IN INDIA

I didn't have to *have it all together*

LILY NEWMAN

I didn't think any more of it until I came across a full-page article in the Manchester Evening News about Cameron Dante, WWMT's front man at the time. His story was amazing – he'd lived this hedonistic lifestyle of DJing and drugs and yet he'd become a Christian when he'd been dragged along to church.

I read the article down the phone to my brother and he challenged me to go along to the church it mentioned – St Mary's in Cheadle. My brother can be a real pain in the proverbial if there's something that he wants you to do, so I rang the church on a Saturday afternoon, hoping there would be no one there and I would get off the hook. But someone did pick up – a vicar who said that the WWMT were playing the next night and did I want to come?

My only experience of church up until that point was twin-sets and pearls, so I went along the next night wearing my best Laura Ashley suit. When I saw the lines of young people queuing up outside in baggy pants and trainers, I thought I'd better just keep on walking. But the vicar I'd spoken to saw me and welcomed me in.

"Who's in the house? God's in the house!" It was phenomenal. I knew straight away that this was a faith that could speak to me. God wasn't some ancient deity – he

story 16

was right here right now. When Cameron did an altar call I went to the front, in tears, totally filled with God. He told me I should check out a kind of Alpha course in a "happening" church near where I lived.

The big thing for me was seeing that I didn't have to have it all together before I started a relationship with God. I was touched by the stories of Cameron's messy life, and yet God had met him and loved him. There were lots of challenges for me in the early days of my faith and I was blown away by the love and support I received from my new Christian family.

Since then, God has used me to help with Message projects and to help set up Act4Africa, a charity rooted in faith which has run HIV stigma reduction and health education programmes for over a million young people in East Africa. My work now is all about helping people in business to overcome their life-limiting scripts and reach their full potential – and my faith has played a huge part in that.

Ian Hamilton

Twenty years of The Message, what a wonderful milestone. I've had the privilege of knowing Andy pretty much all this time. Firstly as Heavyfoot of WWMT and more recently OBE and every stage in between!

Constant throughout has been Andy's passion to tell, through all means, the gospel of Christ to the lost, but equally his unwavering commitment to the marginalised both at home and abroad. Andy and The Message have been a huge encouragement and support to me and Compassion, but that's not where our journey began!

I spent my first thirty working years in the Christian music business and in the final decade of that chapter I first came across Andy and WWMT. The Tribe were into their second album *Dance Planet* which had come out in the US through N'Soul. Some friends and I had started Alliance Music and we took on distribution in UK and Europe for N'Soul. It was the start of a great time together, and in record sales terms a really successful one on both sides of the Atlantic. The Tribe along with Delirious became the UK's leading Christian artists of that decade. Together under Zarc Porter's sonic skills we put together a number of albums with songs that became anthems – *Jumping in the House of God* to name just one. Not one for a ballad, Heavyfoot belted them out!

I think it was during this time I recognised Andy's skills and passion as a fundraiser. The Message had started from humble beginnings around the same time and I recall many conversations with Andy on 'production advances', some of which was spent on making a record and a lot on doing the work of The Message! Nevertheless the records still sounded pretty good!

When I left Christian music to develop the work of Compassion UK in the early 2000's I sought Andy's help. Up to that time he couldn't get his head out of The Message's work in Manchester, but he and Michele somewhat reluctantly came on a trip to Haiti... and the rest is history. Manchester will always be the centre of what Andy's about, but his skills, passions and vision today go way beyond.

What a privilege it's been to walk shoulder to shoulder together in our many ventures these past twenty years. I thank God for Andy and Michele and for the opportunity to call them friends and co-labourers for Christ, truth and justice.

CHIEF EXECUTIVE OF COMPASSION UK

TO DATE, THERE HAVE BEEN OVER

2,000,000 DOWNLOADS

OF THE PODCASTS WE PRODUCE

THE MESSAGE PODCAST

MENU

CHAPTER SEVEN

What Transformation Looks Like

ABOVE LEFT:
OUR SHARSTON
HQ.

ABOVE RIGHT:
HOW THE
BUILDING NEXT
DOOR LOOKED
BEFORE WE GOT
THE KEYS

CENTRE: ANDY
AND ROB TOUR
WHAT WILL
BECOME MESSAGE
HQ

BELOW:
ANDY
HAWTHORNE
AT THE HQ IN
CHEADLE 1994

It wasn't hard to outgrow Mark Pennells' bedroom in which Message to Schools started life. As soon as we started to employ staff and need more administration it was clear we needed more space, so we were delighted when St Andrew's Church in Cheadle Hulme kindly offered us the upstairs room at their vicarage. The room could be accessed via the fire escape which was particularly convenient because it had a small 6ft x 6ft platform at the top which became my office. Whenever I needed space to prepare a message I would pull a curtain across whilst the rest of the team would tiptoe around the room.

It was good to move into Cheadle Mill in 1997 and have three floors of accommodation, but to be honest it was still a slightly ramshackle setup. Cheadle Mill was also quickly outgrown so in 2000 we started to look for a more permanent home with room to grow. One of our business supporters had made us the unbelievably generous offer of buying us a new HQ which would meet our requirements. The deal was amazing: we'd get to rent it for the same price we were paying for the old Mill. We found the ideal place in Sharston and managed to agree a price when, to our surprise, the deal fell through. I was more than a little disappointed that the owners had decided to stay put in what I had felt was the perfect place for us. I spent the next few months

visiting slightly inferior places to the one I had really set my heart on. I clearly remember driving down the A34 one morning early in 2001, and in my mind saying "Lord I'm sure that Sharston building was right for us and none of the ones I've seen since seem half as good." Later that afternoon the phone rang, and it was the owner asking us if we would like to still buy the Sharston building. We then got on enthusiastically with the job of refurbishing and transforming our new headquarters to include all the things we'd dreamed of: offices, warehousing, recording studios, rehearsal rooms and more. What a blessing it was to move into it in 2002.

Next to our new HQ was an empty building owned by the council and it wasn't long before I got to thinking that one day this could be ours. You see I firmly believe that healthy things grow. Occasionally there will be pruning for growth, and growth for the sake of growth is hopeless, but if we are not reaching a whole lot more young people in twenty years than we are today then something will have gone badly wrong. With growth comes the need for more support, more training and administration and so I felt sure that the building next door was being saved for us, especially as it seemed like the only one of its kind for miles around. I made some enquiries at the council and despite them saying they liked what we were doing, they also said they were unable to do us a good deal and would be putting the building up to competitive sealed bids in the very near future. This was right at the height of the property boom and so there

> "I felt sure that the building next door was being saved for us"

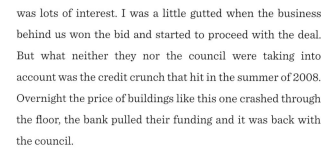

JUNE 2011

was lots of interest. I was a little gutted when the business behind us won the bid and started to proceed with the deal. But what neither they nor the council were taking into account was the credit crunch that hit in the summer of 2008. Overnight the price of buildings like this one crashed through the floor, the bank pulled their funding and it was back with the council.

In the intervening period lots of things had happened and I felt like I knew exactly how we could best use the building. It was all down to what I can only describe as a real move of God, specifically through our work in the area's young offenders' institutions. Through our Reflex prison teams around 40 or 50 young offenders were committing their lives to Christ each month, and while they were inside were making amazing strides in their new faith. It started to become a regular occurrence to hear of these most broken, dysfunctional and previously thoroughly bad young people praying for their friends leading them to Christ in their cells. We'd even heard of some quite remarkable miracles taking place. But of course the hard part comes when it is time for their release. It was desperate to see so many of them sent to live in totally inappropriate hostels, back to chaotic home lives or even on to the streets. As a result many of them ended up falling back into their old lives of addiction and crime when we knew God wanted something so much better for them.

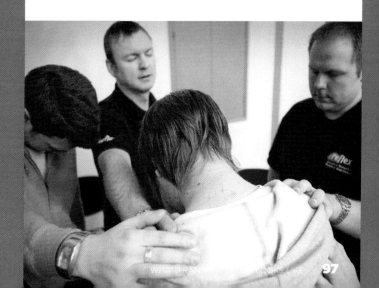

It felt a lot like those early days of Eden in Benchill. What we needed was a pragmatic response to a move of God, some practical help to back up the great things God had done. Over the years we'd concluded that if you can give ex-offenders just three things they'll have a chance of becoming the best they can be: supportive Christian community – and our Eden teams were well placed to deliver that. Decent housing – we were now in touch with a couple of housing providers who were offering to buy houses for us close to our Eden teams. And work – because the key to people thriving is work. We were made to work; with work comes dignity, self-worth and the opportunity to provide for ourselves and our family. I knew that if we could provide all this in a mentoring environment right next to our HQ we really could deliver something beautiful.

So there you have it: in our 20th year we are going for it. The council has done us an amazing deal on the building which we will turn into an enterprise hub. It will house at least six of our businesses which will employ up to fifty ex-offenders in real jobs with real bonuses if they succeed. We believe it will help to incubate businesses around the city.

As we are seeing drug dealers and loan sharks come to Christ, they're bringing with them plenty of entrepreneurial talent as well as the knowledge of how to deal with large amounts of money and employ lots of people but who were previously a nightmare. What a massive win it will be if we can release and support them to run God-honouring businesses all over the city! As the project gets off its feet we will also be working to place ex-offenders in other businesses who have a heart for this and who we believe will give these young men and women a chance to flourish.

I hope you agree it's a thrilling vision. We are aware that there will be many challenges along the way, but we are also convinced that if we can pull it off here in Manchester there is huge potential to see Message Enterprise Centres up and down the country in future years.

IN 2012 THE DOORS WILL OPEN ON THE ENTERPRISE CENTRE. THE ABOVE ARTIST'S RENDERS GIVE AN IDEA OF WHAT THE INTERIOR WILL LOOK LIKE.

THE MESSAGE ENTERPRISE VISION

SUPPORTIVE CHRISTIAN COMMUNITY

A DECENT HOME

GOOD HONEST WORK

Roy
Crowne

The Message was born during my time at Youth for Christ, through a tribe of young people who were passionate about communicating the gospel in a culturally relevant way, with amazing antics on stage.

Together with Soul Survivor we initiated Festival:Manchester and Hope '08 which had a profound effect on Manchester and on the nation as a whole. This was achieved through what we understand to be two sides of the same coin – the words of Jesus, together with the actions of Jesus. It has meant mobilising thousands of young people to do acts of kindness, but never backing off from the story.

Some people would immediately think of gospel preaching when reflecting on The Message. However, the amazing thing about The Message's journey over 20 years, with all its courage, drive, passion and focus, is the way it has interpreted the gospel to this generation of young people. The verse 'faithful in a little and you will be faithful in much' is so relevant as far as The Message is concerned.

The Message continues with fresh vision and faith, 'to go where no one has gone before', out of obedience to God's word to them, going into some of the toughest and most vulnerable areas of society. It would be true to say that they have caught something of God's favour on the journey. Their passion for the next 20 years could be summed up by one of the foremost heroes of the faith, William Booth in his 'I'll fight' sermon. You can sense that The Message is one such tool in the hand of God to bring about Jesus' message of words and actions.

It has been fantastic to partner with them, to have a personal friendship with Andy, and now to serve together in Hope.

EXECUTIVE DIRECTOR OF HOPE TOGETHER

A celebration

of God's amazing work

NICK & ANDREA SHAHLAVI

I was part of a world of drugs and violence from my early teenage years. I was raised by a good mum who did her best, but I found it hard to come under any kind of authority and stick to the rules. I had a lot of anger and I just fell into drugs. It got heavy – dealing, career criminals, kidnappings, beatings, death threats, suicidal behaviour, crack and coke addiction.

I also had a gambling habit which made me a familiar face in casinos around Manchester. One night I met a girl who was dishing out change named Andrea. Things moved fast – before I knew it we were living together, then we had a baby daughter.

But things were about to take a dramatic turn for me. With the help of The Message team, my heart was turned around by God. The power of God transformed my life, renewed me inside and set my heart on fire for other people in the same predicament as I was in.

After a run of bad jobs, I was invited to become an intern with Reflex. It started out as a short-term placement but it became a full-time job running courses and outreach work with convicted young offenders. I found my story was inspirational to lots of the guys I was meeting on the wings. I was a walking testimony of how God can change a life.

But even though the change in me was obvious to other people, Andrea wasn't so sure. It freaked her out that I'd gone from being a drug dealer to a Christian. She thought I was a religious weirdo and she didn't know what to do with me. Things at home got strained, with fights and arguments between us. I'm very glad my daughter Alexis was too young to remember those days.

The turning point for Andrea came when she struck up a friendship with Jane Sullivan, a part-time Message staff member and wife of Simon, who leads the Reflex team. Jane invited her on a mission trip to Uganda and The Message supported us all the way. While she was out there, Andrea encountered the power of God for herself. She came back a changed girl – and she wanted to get married! The only thing was paying for the wedding. But suddenly donations started come in from everywhere... God is a true reconciler.

Our wedding in Autumn 2011 was a celebration of our relationship and God's amazing work in our lives. We just wanted to glorify God for what he's done.

ABOVE: NICK, ANDREA AND BEST MAN ANDY

STACEY MURRAY

Reflex **supported me**
every step of the way

I had a tough start in life: my relationship with my family broke down and I was put into care aged 11. I had a good family but I was a terror and I don't know why. I think maybe I just never felt loved by my mum so I used to kick off all the time and they couldn't handle me.

Even though I left school with no qualifications, I found work quite easily and things seemed to be settling down. But everything collapsed when my boyfriend introduced me to heroin – it took over my life and got me fired from my job. I turned to shoplifting and burglary to fund my habit. Eventually obviously I was caught and sentenced.

I spent nine years in prison on five separate convictions. It was like a revolving door – I'd be out and back in. I had no support. Each time I had every intention of staying off heroin, but I never did. I would smoke on the first day I was out, and I was back at square one.

But on my last sentence, I finally found the help I needed. I became a Christian through Bible studies run by the Reflex team working in HMP Styal and discovered the unconditional love and acceptance I needed. The closer I got to God, the more I changed. He filled that hole I'd been looking to fill for years, using drugs, trying to impress people. I finally knew that I was fully wanted.

Prison never worked for me, until I became a Christian. Then I started to make it work for me. I did lots of courses and I used the time well. Reflex supported me every step of the way, giving me the strength

I needed to deal with life outside, finding a job, getting a flat and settling into a church.

I was released as a Priority and Prolific Offender (PPO) because of my past. It means they watch you much more closely. But my probation officer was so impressed with my new attitude I was released from the scheme within seven months, which at the time was the quickest on record.

I've been out for over two years now. I look back and think: who was that person? I can safely say if I hadn't met the Reflex team and become a Christian, I'd have been in and out of prison for the rest of my life. I couldn't have done it without them.

story
18

Pete Greig

For twenty years, The Message have been breaking all the rules, and I've been doing my best to cheer them on for a fair chunk of that time. Why?

Because of the way they combine social justice with courageous proclamation of the gospel when most people only do one and not the other.

Because of the way they've stayed focused primarily on Manchester and on teenagers, even when Christendom started wolf-whistling from across the pond.

Because of the way they've incarnated the everlasting gospel of Jesus in ever-changing fashions from those early Lady Di braces to baggy, camouflage skater pants to the terror that is fluorescent Lycra. The Message has simply refused to sully the reputation of Jesus with boredom or irrelevance.

Because they've always been focused on the most broken and the most lost when it would have been easy to surf the Christian circuit.

Because they've got their hearts in heaven and their feet firmly earthed in the real world; they're unreligious and able to have a laugh.

I'm also a fan because of the way they've combined big events (make that massive festivals) with grass-roots, long-term, organic, relational presence. Hardly anyone does both well the way The Message does.

And I love the way their vision is always growing and yet somehow (and it can only be the grace of God) they haven't burned out. Andy is generous, focused and irrepressibly full of faith.

The last twenty years have been so much fun. One time I preached at an Eden community and a lad in the front row chose to spend most of my talk saluting me with his middle finger. Another time I had the privilege of staying in a house on a street where every other window was boarded up but the Eden team was bringing life. I've loved times of prayer with the Message staff when they've all been weeping and cheering and yelling and crying out to God. I remember Sunday lunch with one of their leaders. Afterwards he put on his coat and went to take a new Christian to rehab. Isn't that precisely what church leaders should be doing on Sunday afternoons?

At this key milestone it's appropriate to look back and celebrate the goodness of God and to give credit where it's due. But if I know Andy Hawthorne he's already getting fidgety, distracted by something on the horizon and he's already setting off up the road, with a big grin yelling back at us: 'C'mon!'

FOUNDER OF 24-7 PRAYER

THAT'S LIKE DRIVING AROUND THE WORLD 3 TIMES

OUR EDEN
BUSES HAVE
TRAVELLED

75,000

MILES IN
& AROUND
MANCHESTER

eden bus

JODEY ALLEN

One day they asked me what I wanted to pray for and I said **"FORGIVENESS"**

Growing up, I was always in and out of family care. I had a mother who never showed any love towards me. My school said I had behaviour problems but I was just crying out for help.

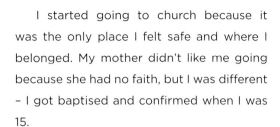

I started going to church because it was the only place I felt safe and where I belonged. My mother didn't like me going because she had no faith, but I was different – I got baptised and confirmed when I was 15.

Things were good for a while until my mum kicked me out of the house and told me to never come back! I ended up in a bad fight with my mother which ended with the police being called and me being arrested.

That's where things started getting really difficult. I forgot about God and was so angry and started getting drunk with my mates all the time. At 17 I was sexually assaulted – it still haunts me. I gave up, self-harmed, drinking out of control. I lost years of my life off the rails.

In June 2010, I did something really stupid and ended up in prison on a 12-month sentence. While inside, I met the Reflex team on an arts and crafts course but I started getting angry when they brought God into things and I withdrew from the group.

Still, they invited me to the Bible study groups on Tuesdays. I started attending and began to open up.

One day they asked me what I wanted to pray for and I said "forgiveness". I wanted to pray for all the people who had hurt me, so they could find God themselves and know that I forgive them.

From that day there was a massive change in me! My faith started to grow more and more each day. I was happy again. I realised God had helped me get through the hard times.

I got released in June 2011 after six months, feeling so much more positive about my future. After only a few weeks I got a job working with YFC (Youth For Christ), sharing God's Word with other people. My faith is stronger than ever and I'm no longer ashamed to say I'm a Christian.

If it wasn't for the Reflex team my faith wouldn't have been brought back to me. I really appreciate it and all that you are doing for me.

story 19

JODEY WITH HANNAH FROM THE REFLEX PRISONS TEAM (ALSO ABOVE)

I want to leave all that stuff *at the cross*

ADAM FOUNTAIN

By the time I hit my twenties, things had got so bad for me in Wythenshawe, I had to get out. I was up to my eyeballs in debt and being chased by violent men – I was deep in the drugs scene and battling my own addiction at the same time.

So I escaped to the North East in the hope no one would catch up with me. But someone did – Jesus. I'd only been there two days when I met some guys who started telling me about him. They started praying for me, and I had this amazing rush all through my body. It was better than any drugs I'd ever had. I gave my life to Christ and immediately wanted to start telling others about him. We were seeing people healed and set free on the streets.

But it didn't last. A few months later I got laid off a job which was helping me get my life back on track. I was down, depressed and my pride was broken. It brought up all the issues I had from when I was younger. So I hit self-destruct again: one night I went wild and I knocked two lads out so badly I knew I'd get sent down.

So I ran – again. But back in Manchester, the Holy Spirit was still on my case. I got on my knees and repented. I said to God, "I want to leave all that stuff at the cross and move on with you... But if a prison sentence is what it takes for me to get back on track with you, then amen." In the end I drove back to Newcastle and handed myself in.

I was convicted of two counts of GBH but some CCTV evidence meant I got let off a prison stretch. I was given a two-year suspended sentence, a large fine and 180 hours of community service instead. They sent me to work on clearing the derelict site that just so happened to be the site of the new Message Enterprise Centre, though I didn't know it at the time.

One morning, I felt God prompting me to go into the next door office and on my next break that's what I did. I met some guys from the Reflex team who helped me get back on track with Jesus and plugged into a great church.

I thought that what I had done would have separated me from the love of God but he's cleaned me up, healed my heart, and delivered me from all that bad stuff. He's so gracious and merciful. I can't wait to see how God uses the new Enterprise Centre to do the same in other lives like mine.

story 20

MATTY HAWTHORNE FROM THE REFLEX PRISONS TEAM IS HELPING TO DISCIPLE ADAM

CHAPTER EIGHT

For All We Know, This is Just the Beginning...

I remember being asked a while ago what my favourite verse in the Bible was. How can you answer a question like that? The Bible is a living book which means that my favourite verse probably changes every day. But on that occasion I said Ephesians 3:20: "Now to him who is able to do immeasurably more than all we ask or imagine according to his power at work in us..."

Isn't that an amazing truth? God is able to do vastly more, not just than the things we dare ask for out loud when we are full of faith, but even more than the desires and dreams of our hearts. And not only that but he chooses to do it in partnership with ordinary, frail, inconsistent people like me and you. I guess that's our story over the last twenty years: God has consistently done more than we've asked for. In fact, he's often immeasurably more than our dreams. Why? Because the gospel is a seed, and when that seed is planted in someone's heart and in their life it has unlimited potential for multiplication.

> "I guess that's our story over the last twenty years: God has consistently done more than we've asked for"

Who could have possibly thought that when we set up Message to Schools in Mark's spare bedroom that over the next two decades we'd see millions of young people's lives touched? Who could have thought that so many ministries would be initiated and that things would spread out all over the world? Well, it's happened and it is totally to God's glory. Of course thinking about all this gives us great confidence and great excitement about the future. What we've experienced over the last two decades is a base from which God will once again delight in doing more than we ask or imagine. And I'm completely confident that if I could get a glimpse now of the 40th year anniversary book we would be astounded with all that God is planning to do through us!

Obviously I don't know it all, but if I could use one phrase to describe the next season and the big vision of the Message it would be 'the multiplication of disciples'. We are believing for so much more than young people giving Jesus a high five at our events; we're believing for these seeds to be planted increasingly in good soil so that, as Jesus put it, they go on all the way with a good and noble heart and themselves produce a bumper harvest. There really is nothing more exciting than seeing that happen in the lives of people who once were some of the most broken that you could imagine.

There are three areas in the next season where I think this multiplication will take place.

GENETIK

Firstly, Genetik, our youth leader training scheme. It's amazing to see the difference that can be made in a person's life through one year of intensive worship, teaching and ministry, especially when it's delivered alongside the opportunity to develop skills and put it all into practice day in and day out. In the next season we are really looking to step this up and be much more strategic by partnering with key friends around the world.

Our plan is to bring gifted young men and women to Manchester for a year and let them catch our DNA while they take part in our team life. We want to get them resourced with the right music, sketches, presentations and passion to take the gospel out all over the world. We will keep a strong link with these teams and do all we can to resource and encourage them as they go out. Our dream is that in the next years there will be dozens of Message associate teams all over the world.

EDEN

LEFT:
THE ANNUAL
EDEN AWAY
DAY 2010

STACY MURRAY
IN THE M.E.C.
READ HER
STORY ON
PAGE 102

M.E.C.

The second key area of multiplication of disciples is Eden. In a few years' time we will have nine fully functioning Eden hubs delivering dozens and potentially hundreds of Eden teams to bring transformation to our nation's toughest estates. This network will have the potential to reach 95% of Britain's most deprived areas, and hopefully it will start to develop other Message-type ministries up and down the country.

Wouldn't it be amazing to see Eden giving birth to schools teams, bands and prison teams? If the area called for it, how about buses, enterprise centres and local training schools up and down the country? We want to do all we can to encourage and resource others who have a similar heart but who might be working outside of our particular Eden hotspots to deliver just that. Whether in the UK or abroad, we're convinced that things are going to multiply.

Thirdly there's our new enterprise hub, The Message Enterprise Centre. It's still just a dream at the moment, and right now we're concentrating on fundraising and starting to transform the building next door to something fit for purpose. But it's a dream that I'm convinced God loves and as such I fully expect to see multiplication kick in: multiplication of kingdom businesses providing great jobs, multiplication of great ministries up and down the country and a multiplication of entrepreneurial disciples literally doing the business for him.

It's all good stuff and there's all the potential in the world. As the guy who leads it I'm so privileged to be able to say that I wouldn't want to do anything else anywhere in the world for any amount of money. How many people can say that with their hand on their hearts?

THE M.E.C. NO LONGER LOOKS LIKE SOMETHING FROM THE DAY OF THE TRIFFIDS

OUR CORE VALUES

Recently I've been thinking not just about the vision for a multiplication of disciples but also about our values. Organisations aren't just shaped by exciting visions – the values that underpin them provide a vital foundation. Our values started in the hearts of a couple of us over twenty years ago, and today we continue to hold on to those values in every aspect of our work.

PASSION

Someone said that when work commitment and pleasure become one, you reach that deep well called passion, and there nothing is impossible. That's the place we are at. I think it's fair to say that The Message is full of very average people – I'm one of them. The only thing that's extraordinary about us is our passion: passion for Jesus, for the poor, lost and hurting, and for the good news. Anyone who looks back at history knows that the only people who have ever really changed the world for God are the ones who were full of passion.

CHURCH

Over the years there's been the occasional temptation to think about setting up a Message denomination. But I can now say, hand on heart, that it's never going to happen. We stand or fall on our partnership with local churches. We don't need more denominations, we just need the ones we've got to become more missional and focus more intently on transforming communities and making the main thing, the main thing. If we can play a part in doing that through being faithfully committed members of local churches and bringing more resources and encouragement to these churches – then, result!

COMMUNITY

It's struck me that every truly world-changing organisation – right back to when the Master said, *"I don't call you servants but friends"* – has been run by a bunch of mates. I want accountable, encouraging friends who don't sit around drinking beer bewailing with me the fact that the nation is going to the dogs. I want to be a part of a community that spurs me on to actually play my part in changing the world for the better in Jesus' name. That's the Message at its best.

INNOVATION

Flexibility has been, and will be, a hallmark of the next twenty years. We must duck and dive and try lots of things in order to bring maximum glory to Jesus and maximum blessing to his world. Yes, sometimes we'll fail. But if we do we just dust ourselves off and try something else. As long as all the innovation and flexibility is born out of passion for God, his word and his world rooted in local churches and worked in good accountable friendships, then I honestly believe that anything goes.

Let's end by coming back to the verses that God spoke to me right at the start of this adventure: *"See, I am doing a new thing! ...do you not perceive it?"* The truth that Isaiah 43 expresses is that God hasn't run out of ideas to see the great commission fulfilled; he's just on the lookout for obedient people who will see and perceive the plans he reveals and get on with living them out. As I look forward to the next twenty years – and as we try and do just that – one thing's for sure: it's going to be an interesting ride!

Rev. Nicky Gumbel

What's so impressive about The Message Trust is its relentless focus on young people who traditionally it has been hardest to reach – especially those living in disadvantaged communities and in prison.

Since the beginning I have followed and admired the passion with which The Message has taken the gospel to the streets of Greater Manchester in word and actions. Just as impressive is their commitment to long-term relational evangelism through Eden. Recently we have been thrilled to be part of the story, partnering with new Eden projects in London and helping support and resource the vision nationally as much as we could.

At the centre of all this is an amazing guy, Andy Hawthorne, who over the last 20 years has led the way with astonishing conviction and energy. The OBE he received from the Queen last year was a fitting tribute to his pioneering work.

VICAR OF HOLY TRINITY BROMPTON & AUTHOR

4,000,000

COPIES OF
WORD 4U 2DAY,
THE DISCIPLESHIP RESOURCE PRODUCED
IN PARTNERSHIP WITH UCB,
HAVE BEEN PRINTED

CHAPTER NINE

Twenty Years, Twenty Legends

It's been an impossible task picking twenty people who represent the passion and vision that has carried The Message Trust along for the past twenty years, and I'm confident that there are at least 20,000 glaring omissions, probably including you! So, thank you once again to all of you. Here's a tiny selection of just some of the fun-filled people we have been privileged to work with over the past two decades.

Andy Hawthorne

LEGEND 1 – Val Grieve was a Manchester solicitor and a passionate follower of Jesus who was my mentor as a baby Christian in the late 1970s. He constantly spurred me on to reach the lost and the hurting and he was involved in pretty much everything significant that was happening in the city, including Billy Graham's visit to Maine Road in 1964. When we started the trust, Val found us £5,000 that was left over from this Billy Graham visit and gave us our first major donation. He went to heaven in 1998.

LEGEND 2 – Mike Spratt runs Wigwam Acoustics – a P.A. company originally born out of Heywood Baptist Church that has gone on to provide P.A. for some of the world's most successful artists, including Coldplay, George Michael and the Spice Girls. He was the first person my brother phoned when we had the idea for Message '88 and since then he has consistently gone way beyond the call of duty in providing the most excellent gear for numerous Message events.

LEGEND 3 – Liza Fawcett's story received a full page in the Manchester Evening News. She heard me speak about Eden at New Wine and felt God's call to move from her cottage in the poshest postcode in Britain – Chorleywood – to serve in what was then officially the most deprived area in the country, Harpurhey.

LEGEND 4 – Dave Aston. At the very start of this whole adventure I remember being astounded when Dave sent us a cheque for £1,000 in support of Message '88. I was amazed that anyone would believe in our vision that much. It was the first of many cheques that he would send us, accompanied by multiple thousands of hours volunteering, setting up equipment so that young people could hear the gospel, before later joining our full-time Operations team in 1999.

LEGEND 5 – My Mum. It may seem a bit cheesy but I'm convinced that there would not be a Message Trust without Christine Hawthorne. Not just because of her unbelievable passion and daily prayer for what we do but also her ability to recruit, in so many different ways, volunteers to serve faithfully behind the scenes.

LEGEND 6 – Alison Hudson.
Every week until she went to be with the Lord in 2004 we would receive a long encouraging letter from Alison, accompanied by a £5 or £10 note from her pension. She prayed her socks off for The Message and she was part of my mum's letter-stuffing team. She believed we were the answer to a promise that God had given her back in the 1940s that there would be a major move of God amongst young people in the UK.

LEGENDS 7-8 – Richard & Sylvia Johnson.

It is quite hard and perhaps not quite totally fair to pick one of our trustees for this legend status, but Richard has been the Chairman of The Message Trust since the very beginning. He's never once looked to quash our faith or limit our plans, no matter how outrageous the ideas have become. Alongside every great man there tends to be a great woman like Sylvia. She shares Richard's passion and has served in numerous voluntary capacities over the past twenty years.

LEGENDS 9-10 John & Rose Lancaster
first sent us a cheque for £100 after watching the 'Get God' discipleship video back in 1994. Little did we know that over the next 18 years God would grip their hearts with the work of The Message and that they would go on to support Eden Buses, Eden teams, our prisons work, the TLG school in Harpurhey, and much more. They are quite literally two of the most generous people on the planet. Over the years we've grown to love not just their donations but their incredible passion for youth, and specifically broken young people.

LEGEND 11 – George Verwer.

Somehow I have managed to find myself on George's prayer list and I'm so glad I am. George will often phone me just when I need it with a word of encouragement and a challenge to keep going. What I didn't realise was that I am just one of literally thousands of people who get this treatment. Everything within me wants to remain as zealous and focussed on the Lord and the lost and hurting as George is when I am in my 70s.

LEGEND 12 – Sister Jan Rose
is one of our faithful prayer supporters who are the engine room behind everything that we do. Regularly we will receive letters from her encouraging us to keep going. She lives in a tiny garden shed in the Welsh countryside and prays her socks off day in and day out for The Message.

LEGENDS 13-14 – Zarc Porter & Mark Pennells are the musical geniuses behind so much of The Message's output, especially in the early days with The World Wide Message Tribe. Without their commitment to excellence and passion for Christ I really wonder if there would be a Message Trust today. Mark was the visionary behind Message to Schools and left behind the chance of record deals and big gigs with his band to chase the lost and the hurting instead.

LEGEND 15 – Laura Neilson came to Manchester to work on the first five days of Message 2000 on the Swinton Valley Project and has never left. In the months that followed the event she pretty much single-handedly followed up the move of God and eventually became part of the Harpurhey Eden team before falling in love with Chris from the Eden Openshaw team. Together they pioneered Eden Fitton Hill and Laura has also led the remarkable Hope Citadel Christian health centres in Fitton Hill, Failsworth and Middleton.

LEGENDS 16-17 Dave & Colette Nuttall were the very first Eden workers who moved into Benchill in 1996. When they moved into their house most of the other houses on the street were boarded up. Since then boarded-up houses have become a thing of the past. They have brought up their family in the same home, been committed to local church and send their kids to the local school. Dave is chair of governors of three local schools and manager of a local football team, and was a local council candidate. They're playing their part in seeing real change come in Wythenshawe and love living there.

LEGENDS 18-19 – Paul and Gillian Nadin are passionate Jesus followers and another ridiculously generous couple. Paul is a businessman and one of our Message trustees. In 2008 the credit crunch hit and resulted in several of our major donors having to significantly reduce their support. This would have almost certainly meant cutting back on projects and laying off staff had it not been that the last deal the bank did before the crunch: the sale of Paul and Gillian's business. It resulted in the largest single donation ever given to The Message.

LEGEND 20 – Tim Mycock is perhaps the perfect example of The Message Trust in action. He became a Christian after The World Wide Message Tribe visited his school. Then he became a student on our Xcelerate evangelists' training school where he well and truly caught the bug for lost and marginalised young people. He now works full-time on our prisons team and through his efforts by God's grace has seen hundreds of young offenders discover life in Jesus.

To cap it all I was awarded an OBE
in the Queen's birthday honours list.
I collected it with Michele, Sam and Beth
at Buckingham Palace on November 18th 2011.
I'm well aware that this award
is on behalf of thousands of people
who made the last 20-year adventure possible.

Here's to the next 20!

>>>HOW YOU CAN HELP>>>

THANKS FOR BEING PART OF THE STORY.

Everything we've achieved over the last twenty years, we've done together. Together with local churches. Together with other movements who share our heart. And together with people like you, reading these words right now.

The truth is, without the faithful prayers, generous donations and many thousands of volunteer hours, none of what you've just read could have happened.

We thank God for everyone who has stood with us over the last twenty years. Now, will you come with us as we fulfil the dreams we have for the next twenty?

INDIVIDUALS AND FAMILIES...

can pray for us every day, asking God to smile on our work and multiply our efforts. You can join one of our Eden partnerships as a tent-making missionary, sent to be a blessing to some of our toughest estates, or join Genetik, our dynamic ten-month training programme.

Please also give whatever you can afford. A regular monthly donation is the best way to help us plan long term. You may also wish to include The Message in your will, helping leave a legacy of faith for the future.

> To sign up to our weekly prayer email, visit:
> **www.message.org.uk/prayer**

> To explore joining an Eden team, please email:
> **info@eden-network.org**
> or phone **08451 948 668**

> To find out more about Genetik, please email:
> **genetik@message.org.uk**
> or phone **0161 946 2300**

> To arrange a regular gift or to find out more about leaving a legacy, please contact our Supporter Relations team at:
> **supporter.relations@message.org.uk**
> or phone **0161 946 2300**

BUSINESSES AND TRUSTS...

can play a strategic role in The Message by becoming part of the Message Business Network (MBN) – a group of executives and business owners donating both finance and business acumen to help us achieve our goals. You could also serve as business mentor for fledgling businesses housed in the Message Enterprise Centre.

> To join the Message Business Network, please email:
> **mbn@message.org.uk**
> or phone **0161 946 2300**

> To offer your services to the Message Enterprise Centre, please email:
> **enterprise@message.org.uk**
> or phone **0161 946 2300**

CHURCHES AND COMMUNITY GROUPS...

can partner with us to set up new Edens on needy estates, sending urban missionaries to reach more young people in the toughest places. You can partner with us to run high-impact schools weeks to reach local schools and colleges with the gospel.

And you can support young offenders leaving custody together with our Reflex team.

> To find out about partnering on a new Eden, please email:
> **info@eden-network.org**
> or phone **08451 948 668**

> To learn more about schools weeks, please email
> **bookings@message.org.uk**
> or phone **0161 946 2300**

> To discuss helping reintegrate an ex-offender, please contact
> **reflex@message.org.uk**
> (in the North West) or
> **info@reflex.org**
> (rest of UK)